GoodGame
Legacy Playbook

Published by: Bingham Ventures, LLC
No part of this book may be reproduced, distributed, or transmitted in any form or by any means, including photocopying, recording, or other electronic or mechanical methods, without the prior written permission of the publisher, except in the case of brief quotations embodied in critical reviews and certain other noncommercial uses permitted by copyright law. For permission requests, write to the publisher, addressed "Attention: Permissions Coordinator," at the email address below.

Bingham Ventures LLC
PO Box 81
Union City, GA 30291
charlie.bingham@gmail.com

GoodGame Legacy Playbook: Building Wealth, Winning, and Securing Generations
1st edition, August 2024
Paperback ISBN: 978-1-7372501-4-2

The content of this book is provided for informational purposes only. The author and publisher have made every effort to ensure the accuracy and completeness of the information presented. However, they assume no responsibility for errors, omissions, or contrary interpretation of the subject matter herein.

The information contained in this book is not intended as a substitute for professional advice. Readers should seek the advice of qualified professionals regarding specific questions or concerns. The author and publisher shall not be held liable for any damages or losses, directly or indirectly, arising from the use or misuse of the information contained in this book.

All opinions expressed in this book are those of the author and do not necessarily reflect the views of the publisher or any other organization. Any resemblance to actual persons, living or dead, or actual events is purely coincidental.

GoodGame Legacy Playbook:
Building Wealth, Winning, and Securing Generations

CHARLIE BINGHAM JR.

Contents

PREFACE

"The world is filled with talented poor people. All too often, they're poor or struggle financially or earn less than they are capable of, not because of what they know but because of what they do not know."

—**Robert Kiyosaki**, *Rich Dad Poor Dad: What the Rich Teach Their Kids About Money That the Poor and Middle Class Do Not!*

"[T]he goal for successive generations should be self-sufficiency and independence, and so it focuses on the ability to replicate wealth and not simply on sustaining and consuming it. It's based on a simple but fundamental principle: successive generations, when given sufficient opportunity and means, can and will achieve on their own."

—**Garrett B. Gunderson**, *What Would the Rockefellers Do?: How the Wealthy Get and Stay That Way, and How You Can Too*

As I reflect on the words of Garrett B. Gunderson, I'm reminded of the profound truth that lies at the heart of our quest for generational wealth: the ability to replicate wealth, not merely sustain it, is the key to unlocking a future of prosperity for ourselves and our loved ones. Wealth isn't just about money in the bank; it's about opportunities, security, and the ability to build a better future for yourself and your family. Wealth makes it easier for families to invest in their own futures. For example, wealth can be used to support both children's and parents' education, to start a business, to buy a house in a neigh-borhood with access to good jobs, and to move to new places when better opportunities arise. Each of these benefits gives families access to more and better resources. People with higher levels of education typically have lower unemployment rates and greater access to well-paying, stable career options with decent benefits; starting a business gives people more control over their own lives and thus the potential to avoid the uncertainty that can come from working for somebody else in a low-paying job with irregular hours; and buying a house closer to where good jobs are located makes it easier to switch jobs when one does not pan out as expected. Similarly, wealth allows families to move to a new location when jobs or opportunities in one area decline or disappear altogether. All these considerations support the building of generational wealth.

But this journey for African Americans is not without its challenges. From the legacy of slavery and segregation to systemic barriers that persist today, African Americans have faced formidable obstacles in their pursuit of economic empowerment. Imagine a journey stretching back over 160 years, from the aftermath of the Civil War to the present day. Along this path lies a story of struggle, resilience, and a fight for economic justice that continues to shape the lives of African Americans today. African Americans were kidnapped and brought to this country as property, they were enslaved, denied the opportunity to generate income and accumulate wealth and their labor exploited for the benefit of white Americans. Even after slavery ended, discriminatory practices like sharecropping and Jim Crow segregation continued to limit economic opportunities for African Americans, pushing them into poverty and economic oppression.

After slavery, in 1865, Union General William T. Sherman issued Special Field Order No. 15, granting 40-acre parcels of land to newly freed slaves. This bold move aimed to provide a pathway to prosperity for generations to come. However, this promise was short-lived. President Andrew Johnson, this nation's 17th President that assumed the presidency as a Democrat after Abraham Lincoln was assassinated, reversed course, returned the land to white Southern planters, and left African Americans without compensation for centuries of exploitation.

American history tries to make us forget what happened in Greenwood, Tulsa, in 1921. In Greenwood, Tulsa, African Americans came together due to discriminatory policies to form a prosperous African American neighborhood called Black Wall Street. Envious of the success of African Americans, a white mob destroyed it, killing hundreds and stealing millions of dollars of African American wealth.

In addition, Federal policies, such as those enacted during the New Deal and World War II, further entrenched wealth inequality. Programs like the GI Bill and homeownership policies disproportionately benefited white Americans, while excluding or discriminating against African Americans. For example, redlining practices systematically denied African American families access to affordable housing and favorable mortgage terms, making it harder for them to build wealth through homeownership.

Fast forward to the present, where the echoes of history reverberate in the form of the racial wealth gap. Despite significant strides since the civil rights movement, the gap persists, with little progress made since 1950. Babyboomers and Generation X have even encountered policies like those championed by Ronald Reagan. Reagan's economic agenda, often referred to as Reaganomics, favored tax cuts for the wealthy and deregulation, which disproportionately benefited white Americans. These policies led to fewer good-paying jobs for African Americans and increased economic vulnerability. Additionally, tough-on-crime policies enacted during Reagan's presidency fueled mass incarceration, disproportionately affecting African American communities, and devastating African American families economically. While we don't have the time and space to dig into the fallacy of the American "War on Drugs" and the negative impact it has had on African American families, I do recommend that you do some independent research. For a detailed history, I strongly suggest reading "The New Jim Crow: Mass Incarceration in the Age of Colorblindness" by Michelle Alexander.

Yet, despite these challenges, we stand on the shoulders of giants—men and women who dared to dream of a better future and fought tirelessly to make it a reality. In a world marked by unequal access to opportunities and resources, the quest for generational wealth stands as a beacon of hope for African American families seeking to break free from the shackles of economic inequality. It's a journey that spans generations, rooted in the resilience and determination of those who came before us. From the abolitionists and civil rights leaders who paved the way for progress to the entrepreneurs and innovators who continue to shatter glass ceilings, our history is a testament to the resilience and determination of the African American spirit.

In this book, we will embark on a journey toward building

and protecting generational wealth—a journey guided by knowledge, fueled by determination, and inspired by the vision of a brighter future. From education and insurance to financial investment accounts and real estate, we will explore the myriad pathways to wealth creation and preservation available to African American families today. But this book is more than just a roadmap to financial success; it's a call to action—a call to reclaim our rightful place at the table of prosperity and ensure that future generations have the tools and resources they need to thrive. It's a reminder that our wealth is not just measured in dollars and cents, but in the opportunities we create, the legacies we leave behind, and the futures we build for those who come after us.

As we embark on this journey together, I urge you to approach it with an open mind and a steadfast determination to succeed. Let us arm ourselves with knowledge, empower ourselves with action, and dare to dream of a future where generational wealth is not just a possibility, but a reality for all African American families.

Thank you for joining me on this journey. Together, let us build a future where wealth knows no bounds and opportunity is within reach for all. To God be all the glory!

With warmest regards,

Charlie Bingham Jr.

CHAPTER 1:
Empowering African Americans for Financial Success

"Only the man who does not need it is fit to inherit wealth—the man who would make his own fortune no matter where he started. If an heir is equal to his money, it serves him; if not, it destroys him. But you look on and you cry that money corrupted him. Did it? Or did he corrupt his money?

—**Garrett B. Gunderson**, *What Would the Rockefellers Do?: How the Wealthy Get and Stay That Way, and How You Can Too*

IN THE PURSUIT of financial success, African Americans face unique challenges rooted in systemic disparities and historical injustices. Despite significant strides in various fields, the road to building and protecting generational wealth remains fraught with obstacles. From inadequate access to quality education to limited opportunities for economic advancement, the path forward can seem daunting. However, by leveraging education, insurance, financial investment accounts, real estate, and other corporate and financial vehicles, African Americans can overcome these barriers and pave the way for a brighter financial future. In this chapter, we'll explore the tragedy of our miseducation, bridging the wealth gap through financial literacy, and understanding financial resilience and how these areas play a crucial role in securing a prosperous future for you and your loved ones.

The Tragedy of our Miseducation, Untimely and Unfortunate Deaths, and GoFundMe Solicitations

"We are not taught key financial principles," lamented Garrett B. Gunderson in his book, *What Would the Rockefellers Do?: How the Wealthy Get and Stay That Way, and How You Can Too.* This sentiment echoes the reality faced by many African Americans who have been failed by the education system. Instead of equipping us with essential financial knowledge, the system often perpetuates inequality by focusing solely on preparing individuals to be workers. As a result, generations of African Americans have spent their lives working tirelessly, only to find themselves struggling to make ends meet and unable to build wealth.

"We spend so much time working that we fail to spend time learning how to build wealth," Gunderson astutely observed. Indeed, the demands of everyday life leave little room for financial education and planning. With all their hard work, many African Americans find themselves barely able to afford burial expenses, let alone provide financial security for their loved ones. The tragic consequence is a reliance on GoFundMe solicitations to cover funeral costs and other unexpected expenses—a stark reminder of the systemic failures that perpetuate financial instability within our communities.

Empowering Our Future: Transforming Education for Success

The cornerstone of financial empowerment is education. African American high school students are part of an education system designed for a different era—one that prioritized preparing students for factory work rather than equipping them with the tools to build generational wealth. It's time we recognize this discrepancy and demand a shift towards a curriculum that empowers them to thrive in the modern world. It's time to face the truth: the current education system in the United States has let not only African American but also Hispanic and Indigenous folks down. Instead of equipping all students, especially those from African American, Hispanic, and Indigenous communities, with the tools they need to thrive in college, careers, and civic life, it has perpetuated inequality and hindered opportunities for generations. The repercussions of this failure are undeniable. Dropout rates, unemployment, and underemployment rates among these communities far exceed national averages, exacerbating the racial wealth gap. These disparities not only affect economic opportunities but also civic engagement, as communities of color vote at lower rates, resulting in a government less responsive to their needs. To address this disparity, we must advocate for comprehensive reform that prioritizes early exposure to diverse career options, holistic preparation for college and careers, and school accountability aligned with career readiness.

Building Bridges for Success: A Community-Centered Approach

Success requires collaboration across various sectors of society. By fostering partnerships between employers, community organizations, and educational institutions, we can provide students with the skills and experiences needed to succeed. Through academic and civic engagement, we can empower the next generation to drive positive change and shape their own futures. It's time to reimagine education as a catalyst for empowerment and opportunity, breaking the cycle of inequality and building a brighter future for all. By equipping students with the skills, knowledge, and resources they need to succeed in college, careers, and civic life, we can break the cycle of inequality and build a brighter future for every individual. It's time we take control over our own education – even if it means homeschooling our youth!

Bridging the Racial Wealth Gap: Empowering African Americans Through Financial Literacy

Financial literacy emerges as a potent tool for bridging the racial wealth gap. Recent studies underscore a troubling truth: the racial wealth gap persists, with African American families holding a fraction of the wealth compared to their

White American counterparts.[1] According to the Federal Reserve, for every dollar of wealth held by the typical White American family, the typical African American family possesses only around ten cents.[2] This staggering gap highlights the systemic disparities that hinder our economic progress. Data from the TIAA Institute-GFLEC Personal Finance Index reveals a stark reality: on average, African Americans correctly answered only 38% of financial literacy questions.[3] This indicates a significant gap in knowledge that hampers the ability to make informed financial decisions. Additionally, demographic variations show that financial literacy is higher among men, older individuals, and those with more formal education and higher incomes.

Research shows that individuals with higher levels of financial literacy are more likely to engage in prudent financial behaviors, such as retirement planning and avoiding high-cost financial products.[4] In essence, financial literacy serves as a catalyst for realizing our aspirations and securing our family's future. Research has shown that personal finance education helps students avoid payday loans, have better

---

1 Moss, Emily, et al. "The Black-white wealth gap left Black households more vulnerable." Brookings, https://www.brookings.edu/articles/the-black-white-wealth-gap-left-black-households-more-vulnerable/. June 14, 2024.

2 *Id.*

3 Yakoboski, Paul, et al. "Financial literacy, wellness and resilience among African Americans." TIAA Institute, https://www.tiaa.org/public/institute/about/news/financial-literacy-wellness-and-resilience-among-african-americans. June 14, 2024.

4 Yang, Zhen, et al. "Does Financial Literacy Affect Household Financial Behavior? The Role of Limited Attention." Frontiers in Psychology, https://www.ncbi.nlm.nih.gov/pmc/articles/PMC9252460/#:~:text=Research%20on%20Financial%20Literacy%20and%20Financial%20Behaviors&text=Many%20studies%20have%20demonstrated%20that,et%20al.%2C%202022). June 14, 2024.

credit outcomes, and reduce debt burdens.[5] Yet, only 21 states require students to take personal finance coursework to graduate high school, and access to this education remains unequal.[6] In fact, only 7.4% of African American and brown students are required to take a stand-alone personal finance course.[7]

Imagine a world where every African American has access to comprehensive financial education, where schools prioritize teaching personal finance as a core subject. Imagine a future where African Americans are equipped with the knowledge and skills to make informed financial decisions, to invest wisely, and to pass down wealth to future generations. The time to act is now. By investing in financial education and advocating for greater access to financial literacy initiatives tailored to the specific needs of African American communities, we can embark on a journey to unlock our financial potential. We can create a future where the narrative of struggling with money and failing to overcome the barriers that hinder the creation of generational wealth for our community is replaced with one of financial empowerment and success.

The journey begins with understanding the stark realities of the racial wealth gap and the pivotal role financial

5 Fox, Michelle, "Teaching personal finance to kids can help to close the Black wealth gap." CNBC, https://www.cnbc.com/2021/04/06/teaching-financial-literacy-to-kids-can-shrink-the-black-wealth-gap.html. June 14, 2024.

6 Epperson, Sharon, "Making the grade in financial literacy: More states require students to take a personal finance course." CNBC, https://www.cnbc.com/2023/12/05/more-states-require-students-to-take-personal-finance-course.html. June 14, 2024.

7 Fox, Michelle, "Teaching personal finance to kids can help to close the Black wealth gap." CNBC, https://www.cnbc.com/2021/04/06/teaching-financial-literacy-to-kids-can-shrink-the-black-wealth-gap.html. June 14, 2024.

literacy plays in bridging this divide. Financial literacy empowers us to navigate the complex financial landscape, including homeownership, entrepreneurship, and investing. Financial literacy is not just about knowing how to balance a checkbook—it's about empowerment and liberation. By mastering concepts like budgeting, investing, and debt management, we position ourselves to achieve our financial goals and pave the way for future generations. Similarly, understanding the principles of investing can help you grow your wealth over time through avenues like stocks, bonds, and real estate. By investing in your financial education now, you're not only securing your own future but also laying the foundation for generational wealth. Imagine the satisfaction of providing your children and grandchildren with opportunities previously deemed unattainable—a testament to your commitment to breaking the cycle of economic inequality.

Understanding Financial Resilience

With all the time we spend working to make ends meet, we often overlook the importance of learning how to build wealth. As a result, many of us find ourselves struggling to afford even the most basic necessities, let alone think about securing our family's future. It's time to break free from this cycle of financial instability and move toward financial resilience. Financial resilience, the ability to withstand unexpected financial shocks, is crucial for building wealth. However, many African Americans lack this resilience, as evidenced by data showing that 60% of those who answered less than 25% of financial literacy questions couldn't come up with $2,000 within 30 days.[8] This underscores the importance of improving financial literacy to enhance resilience in the face of economic challenges. The racial wealth gap remains a significant challenge, with the median net worth of African American households significantly lower than that of White American households.

The economic landscape reflects a sobering reality, but it's one that should fuel action rather than despair. Addressing the wage disparities alone could uplift an estimated two million African Americans into the middle class, reshaping the trajectory for generations to come. Consider the numbers: the median annual wage for African American workers trails behind their white counterparts by approximately 30 percent, translating to a staggering $10,000 difference.[9] Despite constituting 12.9 percent of the labor force, African American workers only command 9.6 percent of total US wages.[10] Closing the racial wage gap could inject an additional $220 billion annually into African American wages, lifting incomes by 30 percent and bringing one

---

8 Yakoboski, Paul, et al. "Financial literacy, wellness and resilience among African Americans." TIAA Institute, https://www.tiaa.org/public/institute/about/news/financial-literacy-wellness-and-resilience-among-african-americans. June 14, 2024.

9 Chui, Michael, et al. "The economic state of Black America: What is and what could be." McKinsey & Company, https://www.mckinsey.com/~/media/mckinsey/featured%20insights/diversity%20and%20inclusion/the%20economic%20state%20of%20black%20america%20what%20is%20and%20what%20could%20be/the-economic-state-of-black-america-what-is-and-what-could-be-f.pdf. June 14, 2024.

10 U.S. Bureau of Labor Statistics, "Labor force characteristics by race and ethnicity, 2022." BLS Reports, https://www.bls.gov/opub/reports/race-and-ethnicity/2022/home.htm#:~:text=Blacks%20made%20up%2013%20percent,health%20aides%20(33%20percent). June 14 2024.

million more African American workers into employment.[11] It's a concentrated issue, with less than 4 percent of occupational categories accounting for over 60 percent of the wage gap, spanning sectors like professional services, manufacturing, and financial services.[12]

The patterns are clear: African American workers are overrepresented in low-wage occupations and underrepresented in higher-wage ones. Nearly half of African American workers find themselves in healthcare, retail, and accommodation and food services, often in lower-paying service roles. This perpetuates the wage gap, with 43 percent of African American workers earning less than $30,000 per year, compared to the $42,000 median wage for all US workers.[13]

Imagine a future where the racial wealth gap is narrowed, where African Americans have the tools and knowledge to build generational wealth and secure their family's financial future. This future is within reach, and the key to unlocking it lies in financial literacy. By leveraging education, insurance, financial investment accounts, real estate, and other financial vehicles, African Americans can overcome systemic barriers

11 Chui, Michael, et al. "The economic state of Black America: What is and what could be." McKinsey & Company, https://www.mckinsey.com/~/media/mckinsey/featured%20insights/diversity%20and%20inclusion/the%20economic%20state%20of%20black%20america%20what%20is%20and%20what%20could%20be/the-economic-state-of-black-america-what-is-and-what-could-be-f.pdf. June 14, 2024.

12 U.S. Bureau of Labor Statistics, "Labor force characteristics by race and ethnicity, 2022." BLS Reports, https://www.bls.gov/opub/reports/race-and-ethnicity/2022/home.htm#:~:text=Blacks%20made%20up%2013%20percent,health%20aides%20(33%20percent). June 14 2024.

13 Malinsky, Gill, "The racial wealth gap starts as early as 16 for Black workers – and results in 'a lifetime of consequences,' says expert." CNBC, https://www.cnbc.com/2024/02/15/racial-wage-gap-starts-as-early-as-16-heres-why.html. June 14, 2024.

and build generational wealth. The power to unlock generational wealth lies within us—let's embrace it and pave the way for a future defined by economic prosperity and opportunity.

Steps to Enhance Financial Literacy

1. **Seek Reliable Information:** Utilize online platforms, books, podcasts, and organizations tailored to providing financial education for the African American community.

2. **Build a Supportive Network:** Join or create communities of like-minded individuals to share experiences and gain insights from mentors who have achieved financial success.

3. **Take Action:** Develop a financial plan aligned with personal goals, focusing on budgeting, saving, investing, and debt management. Regularly monitor progress and adjust strategies as needed.

CHAPTER 2:
Nurturing Generational Wealth: Smart Financial Strategies

"But there is one distinction that I would like to point out. I've noticed that my friends with money talk about money. And I do not mean brag. They're interested in the subject. So I learn from them, and they learn from me. My friends, whom I know are in dire straits financially, do not like talking about money, business or investing. They often think it rude or unintellectual. So I also learn from my friends who struggle financially. I find out what not to do."

—**Robert Kiyosaki**, *Rich Dad Poor Dad: What The Rich Teach Their Kids About Money That the Poor and Middle Class Do Not!*

IN OUR JOURNEY towards building and safeguarding generational wealth, it's crucial to understand the essence of wealth itself. Is it merely about money, or does it encompass something more profound? Let's delve into the fundamentals, embrace the wealthy mindset, and fortify our financial fortresses against the relentless tide of economic challenges. In this chapter, we will focus on generational wealth, the agenda of financial institutions, and how to overcome systemic barriers to create, grow and preserve generational wealth in securing a prosperous future for you and your loved ones.

Understanding Generational Wealth

Generational wealth isn't just about amassing riches for oneself; it's about orchestrating a symphony of prosperity that echoes through the corridors of time. It involves the strategic transfer of assets, knowledge, and opportunities from one generation to the next, ensuring a legacy of financial security and abundance. Unlike fleeting concepts like financial freedom, which focus on immediate gratification, generational wealth is a beacon of enduring prosperity.

Picture this: It's the timeless tale of a parent bequeathing their earthly possessions to their children, imbuing them with a head start in life. This inheritance becomes a catalyst, propelling successive generations towards greater heights of achievement. It's the power of compounding in action, where wealth begets more wealth, creating an unstoppable momentum that transcends individual lifetimes.

But generational wealth isn't limited to monetary assets alone. It encompasses a diverse array of resources, including businesses, real estate holdings, investment portfolios, life insurance policies, and educational endowments. These multifaceted instruments serve as pillars of stability, fostering intergenerational prosperity and resilience in the face of economic upheavals.

The Agenda of Financial Institutions: Navigating Treacherous Terrain

As we chart our course towards financial empowerment and generational wealth, it's imperative to navigate the complex and treacherous terrain of financial institutions with discernment and foresight. While these institutions tout promises of prosperity, their true agenda often veers towards self-interest rather than communal benefit.

Financial institutions want a slice of the pie too. They'll try to sell you all kinds of dreams, promising to be helpful along the way. But watch out—they're often more interested in their own profits than your long-term wealth. Think about it. In fact, Garrett B. Gunderson stated in his book *What Would the Rockefellers Do?: How the Wealthy Get and Stay That Way, and How You Can Too* that people who hate risk, they put their money in the bank. And in the long run, savings are better than no savings. But it takes a long time to get your money back and, in most instances, you don't get anything for free with it. They used to hand out toasters, but they rarely do that these days.[14]

It is undeniable that financial institutions have a clear agenda:

1. They want our money.
2. They want our money on a regular basis.
3. They want to hold onto our money for as long as possible.

---

14 Garrett B Gunderson, What Would the Rockefellers Do?: How the Wealthy Get and Stay That Way, and How You Can Too, USA, RipWater, LLC, 2016.

4. When it comes time to get our money, they want to pay it back to us as slowly as possible.

Now, let's talk about the financial institution landscape and how it impacts our ability to secure our family's future and build generational wealth. The recent shift to online transactions due to the COVID-19 pandemic has made it even clearer: access to the financial system is crucial for full participation in the U.S. economy. But here's the harsh reality - the system isn't equal for everyone. A critical issue that directly affects your financial future is racial inequity in banking. Despite strides in anti-discrimination laws, people of color, including many of us, still face barriers in accessing quality financial services. Whether it's difficulty in securing loans, facing higher fees, or lacking access to basic banking services, the deck is often stacked against us.

Financial institutions play a crucial role in shaping the economic landscape of our communities, yet there exist stark disparities in access to banking services, particularly affecting African American households. In regions with large municipalities, where demand for banks is high among African American communities, the disparity in access makes things worse. The evidence is clear: despite the myriad benefits of utilizing banks, including increased savings, financial literacy, and access to credit, African American households are disproportionately disadvantaged in accessing these services. Recent studies by Yale SOM and the Federal Reserve reveal that a significant barrier for African American households is the lack of nearby bank branches.[15] This translates into limited access to crucial financial services.

But here's the kicker: it's not just about proximity. While low-income households may have proximity to banks, they exhibit lower utilization rates compared to other groups, possibly due to various factors such as insufficient savings or deep-rooted distrust in financial institutions. Why? It's not because they don't want to or don't see the value. African Americans have had a tumultuous experience with banking in this country. I recommend that you do some research on this. Additionally, the quality and availability of bank branches in African American neighborhoods are often inadequate. Now, you might be thinking, "What's the big deal? Can't I just use online banking?" While digital banking is convenient, many people still rely on in-person interactions at branches. And guess what? African American households are 10% less likely to visit a branch and 7% less likely to use online banking compared to their white counterparts.[16] That's a significant gap.

Contrary to misconceptions, the issue of underutilization among African American households is not primarily driven by lower demand but by limited access to quality bank branches. African American and Hispanic households are disproportionately unbanked or underbanked, facing higher costs for basic financial transactions. The numbers are stark: an estimated 7.1 million households in the United States

---

15 Broady, Kristen, "An analysis of financial institutions in Black-majority communities: Black borrowers and depositors face considerable challenges in accessing banking services." Brookings, https://www.brookings.edu/articles/an-analysis-of-financial-institutions-in-black-majority-communities-black-borrowers-and-depositors-face-considerable-challenges-in-accessing-banking-services/. June 14, 2024.

16 *Id.*

are unbanked, with African American and Hispanic households being disproportionately represented at 13.8% and 12.2%, respectively, compared to just 2.5% of White households.[17] In fact, data shows that in some urban areas, African American households exhibit a higher demand for banking services than their white counterparts, yet this demand is stifled by inadequate access. This disparity extends to credit access, with people of color often facing higher interest rates or outright denials for loans, despite similar financial profiles. The myth that lack of financial education impedes banking utilization is debunked by data showing that individuals resort to alternative financial services for pragmatic reasons, like immediate access to funds amidst income volatility. Consequently, the reliance on alternative financial services, such as check cashers and payday lenders, in African American and Hispanic communities exacerbates the problem. These services often come with exorbitant fees, hindering families from building creditworthiness and accessing affordable credit, which is essential for wealth-building activities like education and entrepreneurship.

Access to credit is fundamental to pursuing opportunities for wealth creation, such as homeownership, education, and entrepreneurship. However, individuals with thin or nonexistent credit histories, often prevalent among low-income and minority populations, face significant hurdles in accessing affordable credit. Even when creditworthy, African American and Hispanic consumers encounter disparities in loan approval rates and interest rates compared to their White counterparts.

The consequences of being unbanked or underbanked

---

17 *Id.*

are profound and perpetuate intergenerational wealth disparities. Without access to mainstream financial services, families are deprived of opportunities to invest in assets that promote long-term financial stability, such as homes and education. Addressing these disparities requires multifaceted solutions. By increasing access to quality banking services, we can level the playing field and empower African American families to take control of their financial futures. One proposed strategy is to integrate banking services into post offices, expanding access for all communities while potentially increasing demand among low-income households. Additionally, policymakers could incentivize banks to establish branches in African American communities through subsidies or tax breaks, thereby narrowing the racial gap in access to banking services.

To further prove the point, recent developments have shed light on discriminatory practices within financial institutions, particularly in mortgage lending. Take, for instance, the case of Bank of America/Countrywide, which settled a Justice Department complaint alleging racial discrimination in mortgage lending.[18] This is not an isolated incident but rather indicative of a larger systemic problem. Research has shown that Bank of America's Countrywide subsidiary was not alone in charging higher rates and fees on mortgages to minorities compared to whites with similar qualifications.[19] This practice, known as "reverse redlining," systematically

---

18 Rothstein, Richard, "A comment on Bank of America/Countrywide's discriminatory mortgage lending and its implications for racial segregation." Economic Policy Institute, https://www.epi.org/publication/bp335-boa-countrywide-discriminatory-lending/#:~:text=Bank%20of%20America's%20Countrywide%20subsidiary,loss%20of%20homeownership%20were%20widespread. June 14, 2024.

19 *Id.*

targeted minority borrowers, pushing them into exploitative subprime mortgages with onerous terms that often led to foreclosure and loss of homeownership.

Consider the statistics: lower-income African Americans were more than twice as likely as lower-income whites to have subprime loans, and higher-income African Americans were about three times as likely as higher-income whites to have subprime loans.[20] This disparity persisted even in communities that were not economically disadvantaged. The fallout from the subprime mortgage resulted in a devastating loss of wealth and exacerbation of racial segregation. The consequences of such discriminatory practices extend far beyond individual homeowners. Foreclosed homes left boarded up in neighborhoods not only lead to declines in property values but also increased crime rates and reduced access to quality education for children. This contributes to the perpetuation of racially segregated, impoverished neighborhoods, leading to poor educational outcomes for minority children and hindering the accumulation of generational wealth.

Home Ownership: How to Create Generational Wealth

You can try to save money or be prudent about paying off debt, but these acts alone won't typically yield significant wealth that can be passed on. A solid saving and investing strategy can add some more money to the pot, of course. But many people find that buying a home is the easiest and best way to create generational wealth. That's because the equity

---

20 *Id.*

in your home will continue to rise as you pay down the principal of your loan and as the market value of your home increases at the same time. On average, you can expect a 4% increase in the value of your home every year—although that's not always the case. The New York Times notes that existing home prices increased by 45% between December 2019 and June 2022, due to the COVID-19 pandemic.[21] Of course, home values do fluctuate, meaning that there is always the potential for a house to lose some value. Even with those blips, however, homeowners tend to create wealth over time. And if you're buying a home with the goal of creating generational wealth, then you're likely viewing the purchase as a long-term investment.

Now, establishing a financial legacy may mean playing the long game, but it doesn't mean you have to buy a home and just sit on it until you can pass it onto your children. That is one approach, but it's not the only one. Many people piggyback off their initial home investment. They may sell the home for a profit and then purchase a larger home. They may even do it and receive a tax break. Or they may choose to improve, upgrade, or expand their home to increase its value. This can be done through a home equity loan, a cash-out refinance, or a home equity line of credit ("HELOC"). These same tools can also be used to purchase an additional home, whether that's a second home, a vacation home, or an investment property that provides an additional stream of income.

All these strategies are possible thanks to that first home

---

21 Shiller, Robert J., " FOMO Helped Drive Up Housing Prices in the Pandemic. What Can We Expect Next?" The New York Times, https://www.nytimes.com/2022/09/28/opinion/housing-prices-pandemic.html. June 14, 2024.

purchase. Now imagine what you can do with the equity in your home after it's been building up for 10, 20, or 30 years. That's why homeownership is often at the crux of any conversation about how to create wealth. There are other benefits to building home equity, too. You can use that home equity loan, cash-out refinance, or HELOC for other purposes. This might be paying off debt, saving for retirement, or taking a bite out of a student loan. Without home equity, many people would have to dip into their savings accounts or retirement accounts if a large, unexpected cost came up, such as a medical bill, home repair, or car purchase. Naturally, credit cards and private loans can help with these purchases as well, but they often carry much higher interest rates than a home loan.

Helping Your Children Achieve the American Dream

Think about it for a second: If the home you own appreciates by about 4% every year, then so too does the cost to buy a home for your kids. Not only do they have to save money, improve their credit score and financial literacy, and worry about interest rates, but many will also face the prospect of being priced out of the homes they want.

Buying a home for the purpose of passing down wealth gives you a few options:

- Your children can live in the home as they save money for their own real estate purchase—a bonus for you if you're yearning to have your kids nearby!
- You can give the home to your children when you're

ready to downsize, or you can will it to them in your estate planning.

- You can use your home equity to help them with a down payment on a new home, thereby easing some of the burden associated with buying a home.

Creating a Stable Life for Future Generations

We've talked about what a home may mean to the next generation (and the one beyond that), but what does it mean for you? It means security, stability, and predictability. If you lock in a 30-year, fixed-rate mortgage, then your monthly payment will never change. This is a big deal as homes appreciate and the cost of rent continues to climb. Knowing what your monthly housing expenses will be frees up your cash for a variety of other uses. If you're still strategizing about how to build wealth, then this extra money can go toward investments like the stock market or a Roth IRA. Or maybe your goal is paying off debt like student loans—whether those loans are yours or your children's. The point is, when you don't have to worry about housing costs increasing, the world is your oyster when you find extra money in your pocket.

Of course, you don't have to worry about saving and investing and leaving as much as possible for future generations all the time. You can use your hard-earned money however you see fit. You can take a trip, buy a major wish list item, or simply start saving away as you watch your net worth grow through your other investments. There is a fine line between preparing for the future and living in the present. Fortunately, the purchase of a home allows you to do both as you enjoy a wonderful place to live while knowing that the dwelling will one day help your children achieve their own dreams. There's nothing a loving parent wants more!

Addressing Systemic Barriers: A Call to Action

While efforts by the Obama Administration to prosecute financial institutions for discriminatory practices was a step in the right direction, much more needs to be done. The $335 million settlement reached with Bank of America, while significant, is insufficient to address the deep-rooted inequities and restore access to homeownership markets for affected families. Corporate pledges to bridge racial economic disparities, particularly in sectors like home lending and small business support, hold promise. However, sustained progress requires a multifaceted approach, combining private sector initiatives with supportive federal policies and Federal Reserve action.

By understanding and addressing the systemic barriers that hinder access to banking services, we can pave the way for greater financial inclusion and economic empowerment, not only benefiting marginalized communities but also fostering greater economic value for financial institutions and society as a whole. Think about it: with better access to banking services, you can start building wealth for yourself and your family. Financial empowerment is the cornerstone of building a secure future and generational wealth. You'll have the tools and resources you need to invest in assets like education, homeownership, and entrepreneurship – opportunities that pave the way for long-term financial stability and prosperity. Closing the gap in banking access is not just a moral imperative but a pathway to a more equitable and prosperous future for all.

In summary, the road to financial empowerment and generational wealth is fraught with obstacles, particularly for communities of color. Racial inequities in banking access, discriminatory lending practices, and disparities in credit access form formidable barriers on the path to prosperity. Yet, amidst these challenges lies an opportunity for collective action and systemic change. By advocating for equitable banking practices, promoting financial literacy, and demanding accountability from financial institutions, we can dismantle the barriers that perpetuate wealth disparities.

CHAPTER 3:
Exploring Building Generational Wealth Through Real Estate Investment

"Real estate is a powerful investment tool for anyone seeking financial independence or freedom. It is a unique investment tool."

—**Robert Kiyosaki**, *Rich Dad Poor Dad: What The Rich Teach Their Kids About Money That the Poor and Middle Class Do Not!*

REAL ESTATE STANDS as a beacon of opportunity in the quest for generational wealth. It offers a path not just to financial security but to enduring prosperity that can span lifetimes. In this chapter, we'll explore how real estate can serve as a cornerstone of your wealth-building strategy, providing avenues for growth, income generation, and long-term stability.

Understanding the Power of Real Estate

Real estate transcends mere shelter; it represents a tangible asset with the potential to appreciate in value and generate passive income. Whether through rental properties, commercial ventures, or strategic investments, real estate offers a myriad of opportunities to grow your wealth and secure your family's future.

Starting Small, Dreaming Big

One of the most appealing aspects of real estate investment is its accessibility. You don't need to be a millionaire to get started; all it takes is a willingness to learn, a strategic mindset, and the courage to take that first step. Begin with modest goals, such as purchasing a duplex or investing in a fix-and-flip property. As you gain experience and confidence, you can gradually expand your portfolio, building your empire one property at a time.

Embarking on Your Real Estate Journey

To embark on your journey to real estate wealth, consider the following steps:

1. **Educate Yourself:** Arm yourself with knowledge by reading books, attending seminars, and seeking guidance from experienced investors. Understanding the fundamentals of real estate investing will empower you to make informed decisions and navigate potential pitfalls.

2. **Choose Your Strategy:** Real estate offers a variety of investment strategies, from buy-and-hold rentals to fix-and-flip renovations. Assess your financial goals,

risk tolerance, and personal preferences to determine the approach that best suits your needs.

3. **Build Your Team:** Surround yourself with a network of professionals, including real estate agents, attorneys, accountants, and contractors. These individuals can provide invaluable guidance and support throughout the investment process, helping you maximize your returns and minimize risks.

4. **Start Early, Stay Patient:** Building generational wealth requires a long-term perspective and a steadfast commitment to your goals. Be prepared to weather market fluctuations, setbacks, and challenges along the way, knowing that consistency and perseverance will ultimately lead to success.

5. **Diversify Your Portfolio:** Avoid putting all your eggs in one basket by diversifying your real estate holdings across different properties, locations, and asset classes. This will help spread risk and ensure greater stability in your investment portfolio.

6. **Trust Your Agent:** A knowledgeable and experienced real estate agent can be an invaluable ally in your investment journey. Lean on their expertise to identify promising opportunities, negotiate favorable deals, and navigate the complexities of the market with confidence.

Strategies for Building Generational Wealth with Real Estate

Real estate offers a multitude of strategies for building generational wealth. Consider the following approaches:

1. **Real Estate Syndications:** Pool your resources with other investors to participate in large-scale commercial or multifamily projects. Real estate syndications offer the opportunity to benefit from professional management and diversified portfolios, yielding substantial returns over time.

2. **Multifamily Properties:** Invest in apartment buildings or other multifamily properties to generate steady cash flow and long-term appreciation. Multifamily investments provide economies of scale and resilience against market fluctuations, making them ideal vehicles for building generational wealth.

3. **Real Estate Investment Trusts (REITs):** Gain exposure to real estate markets without direct ownership by investing in REITs. These publicly traded companies own and manage income-producing properties, offering diversified portfolios and attractive dividend yields for investors.

4. **The Buy, Rehab, Rent, Refinance, Repeat (The BRRRR Method):** Buy, Rehab, Rent, Refinance, Repeat. This strategy involves acquiring distressed properties, renovating them to increase value, renting them out for passive income, refinancing to extract equity, and reinvesting in additional properties. The BRRRR Method allows investors to leverage their capital and scale their portfolios rapidly over time.

Advantages and Disadvantages of Real Estate Investment

While real estate investment offers numerous advantages, it also comes with its share of challenges and considerations:

Advantages:

- **Potential for Appreciation:** Real estate values tend to appreciate over time, providing opportunities for significant capital gains and wealth accumulation.
- **Steady Income:** Rental properties generate regular cash flow through monthly rent payments, offering a reliable source of passive income for investors.
- **Tax Benefits:** Real estate investors can take advantage of various tax deductions, including mortgage interest, property taxes, depreciation, and more, reducing their overall tax liability.
- **Leverage:** Real estate can be purchased with borrowed funds, allowing investors to control large assets with relatively small initial investments and magnify their returns through leverage.
- **Portfolio Diversification:** Real estate provides diversification within an investment portfolio, reducing overall risk and volatility compared to stocks and other asset classes.
- **Tangible Asset:** Unlike stocks or bonds, real estate is a physical asset with intrinsic value, providing a sense of security and stability to investors.

Disadvantages:

- **Illiquidity:** Real estate investments are relatively illiquid, meaning they cannot be easily converted to cash. Buying and selling properties can be time-consuming and costly, limiting flexibility for investors.

- **High Upfront Costs:** Purchasing real estate requires significant capital for down payments, closing costs, and renovations, making it inaccessible to some investors.

- **Maintenance and Management:** Rental properties require ongoing maintenance, repairs, and management, which can be time-consuming and expensive for investors, especially those with multiple properties.

- **Market Risk:** Real estate markets are subject to fluctuations in supply and demand, interest rates, economic conditions, and other factors, which can impact property values and rental income.

- **Legal and Regulatory Risks:** Real estate investments are subject to various legal and regulatory risks, including zoning laws, building codes, landlord-tenant regulations, and environmental regulations, which can lead to fines, lawsuits, and other liabilities.

Building Your Legacy Through Real Estate

In conclusion, real estate investment offers a powerful pathway to building and preserving generational wealth. By leveraging the inherent advantages of real estate, diversifying your portfolio, and adopting a strategic approach to investing, you can create a legacy of prosperity that endures for generations to come. Whether you're just starting out or looking to expand your existing portfolio, real estate has the potential to unlock new opportunities and elevate your financial future. So, take that first step, and embark on your journey to financial empowerment through real estate today. Your legacy awaits.

CHAPTER 4:
Empowering Entrepreneurship: Unleashing Your Potential for Wealth Creation

"Your financial requirements or wants have nothing whatever to do with your WORTH. Your value is established entirely by your ability to render useful service or your capacity to induce others to render such service."

—**Garrett B. Gunderson**, *What Would the Rockefellers Do?: How the Wealthy Get and Stay That Way, and How You Can Too*

IN THE QUEST for generational wealth, entrepreneurship emerges as a powerful vehicle for creating value, seizing opportunities, and transcending financial limitations. Drawing inspiration from timeless wisdom and modern insights, let us explore the transformative power of entrepreneurial spirit in building and safeguarding wealth for African American families. In this chapter, we will cover serving others with purpose, cultivating an abundance mindset, and capitalizing on opportunities by betting on yourself in securing a prosperous future for you and your loved ones.

The Secret of Creating Value: Serving Others with Purpose

At the heart of entrepreneurship lies the principle of value creation—the art of identifying needs, solving problems, and enriching lives through innovative solutions. Value isn't merely about transactions; it's about fostering meaningful connections and leaving a lasting impact on individuals and communities. Value is all about helping people. When you help people, the money will follow. It's all about using your skills and creativity to make a difference in the world. Think about it like this: if you're starting a small business, your main goal should be to help others. When you focus on giving value to your customers, you're on the right path. And whenever you feel stuck, just ask yourself: How can I help my customers even more?

Imagine this: You have a brilliant idea, a product, or a service that addresses a pressing need or fulfills a desire. By sharing this creation with the world, you're not just making money—you're making a difference. Whether it's a small business venture or a groundbreaking innovation, the key is to focus on serving others with authenticity and purpose. When you prioritize adding value to your customers' lives, financial success becomes a natural byproduct of your efforts.

Faith vs. Fear: Cultivating a Mindset of Abundance

In the journey towards entrepreneurship, the battle between faith and fear rages within us. Do you ever feel like fear holds you back from reaching your dreams? Well, it's time to flip the script and choose faith over fear. Fear whispers doubts and insecurities, casting shadows of uncertainty over our dreams. Fear whispers doubts in your ear, telling you that you're not good enough or that you'll fail. But faith? Faith sees opportunities practically everywhere while fear sees risk and disaster. Faith is the beacon of light that illuminates our path, instilling confidence and resilience in the face of adversity. Let's talk about how renewing your mind can help you bet on yourself and achieve anything you set your mind to.

Renewing your mind is the key to overcoming fear and embracing faith. Renewing your mind means changing the way you think. It's about rewiring your thoughts, beliefs, and perceptions to align with abundance and possibility. You remind yourself of your strengths and all the times you've overcome challenges in the past. Instead of dwelling on limitations, focus on your strengths, talents, and past successes. By nourishing your mind with positivity and optimism, you cultivate a mindset of abundance that empowers you to take bold leaps towards your entrepreneurial aspirations.

Looking Around Corners: Seizing Opportunities with Strategic Vision

Entrepreneurship isn't just about chasing opportunities; it's about anticipating them. By looking around corners and envisioning future trends, you position yourself ahead of the curve, ready to capitalize on emerging markets and evolving consumer needs.

Think of entrepreneurship as a strategic game of chess, where each move is calculated, and every decision is informed by foresight and intuition. Whether it's spotting untapped niches, leveraging emerging technologies, or adapting to shifting market dynamics, the entrepreneurial journey demands vision, agility, and a willingness to embrace change.

Preparing to Capitalize on Opportunities: Equipping Yourself for Success

As you embark on your entrepreneurial journey, arm yourself with the tools, resources, and knowledge needed to thrive in the competitive landscape. Invest in your education, cultivate valuable skills, and surround yourself with mentors and peers who inspire and challenge you to reach new heights.

Remember, entrepreneurship is not for the faint of heart. It requires dedication, perseverance, and a willingness to embrace failure as a steppingstone towards growth. But with unwavering faith in yourself, a spirit of service, and a strategic vision for the future, you have the power to transform your dreams into reality and create a legacy of wealth and prosperity for generations to come.

Bet on Yourself

Now, here's the fun part—betting on yourself! It's about taking risks and stepping out of your comfort zone. So, dare to dream, dare to take risks, and dare to bet on yourself. The journey may be fraught with challenges, but the rewards are boundless for those who have the courage to pursue their entrepreneurial passions. Believe in your abilities and trust that you have the power to create the life you want. Whether it's pursuing your passion, chasing your dreams, or simply being yourself unapologetically, bet on yourself every single time. Embrace the spirit of entrepreneurship, unleash your potential, and let your entrepreneurial journey be a beacon of hope and inspiration for generations to come. Don't let fear hold you back from greatness. Choose faith over fear, renew your mind with positivity, and bet on yourself to achieve your wildest dreams. You've got this!

CHAPTER 5:
Exploring Building Generational Wealth with Dividend Stocks

"Why consumers will always be poor. When the supermarket has a sale on, say, toilet paper, the consumer runs in and stocks up. When the stock market has a sale, most often called a crash or correction, the consumer runs away from it. When the supermarket raises its prices, the consumer shops elsewhere. When the stock market raises its prices, the consumer starts buying."

—**Robert Kiyosaki**, *Rich Dad Poor Dad: What The Rich Teach Their Kids About Money That the Poor and Middle Class Do Not!*

IN THE PURSUIT of building and preserving generational wealth, dividend stocks stand out as a time-tested and reliable strategy. They represent more than just financial instruments; they are seeds of prosperity planted today to yield a bountiful harvest for future generations. In this chapter, we will focus on exploring the world of dividend stocks, their significance, types, benefits, and strategies for leveraging them to create and grow wealth that will secure you and your loved one's a prosperous financial future.

Understanding Dividend Stocks: Nurturing Financial Growth

Dividend stocks serve as the cornerstone of many successful investment portfolios, offering a unique blend of income generation, stability, and long-term growth potential. But what exactly are dividend stocks, and why are they integral to building generational wealth?

Defining Dividend Stocks

Dividend stocks are shares of companies that distribute a portion of their earnings to shareholders in the form of dividends. These dividends represent a tangible return on investment, providing investors with regular income payments simply for holding shares in a company.

Exploring Types of Dividends

Dividends come in various forms, each offering distinct advantages and considerations:

1. **Cash Dividends:** The most common type, where shareholders receive a portion of the company's profits in cash. These dividends provide a steady stream of income, akin to receiving a paycheck from your investments.

2. **Stock Dividends:** Instead of cash, shareholders receive additional shares of stock. While this does not provide immediate liquidity, it increases the

investor's ownership stake in the company, potentially enhancing future dividend payouts.

3. **Property Dividends:** Although rare, some companies distribute physical assets to shareholders as dividends. These assets could include real estate, equipment, or other tangible property.

4. **Special Dividends:** Occasional bonuses given by companies during profitable years or asset sales. While not guaranteed, they represent an unexpected windfall for shareholders.

Benefits of Investing in Dividend Stocks

Dividend stocks offer several compelling benefits that make them attractive for long-term investors:

- **Steady Income:** Dividend payments provide a predictable source of income, making them particularly valuable for retirees or individuals seeking passive income streams.
- **Potential for Growth:** Reinvesting dividends can accelerate the growth of your investment portfolio through the power of compounding, allowing you to harness the full wealth-building potential of dividend stocks.
- **Stability:** Many dividend-paying companies are established, financially sound businesses with a history of consistent dividend payments. This stability can help cushion your portfolio during market downturns.
- **Inflation Hedge:** Dividend payments have the

potential to outpace inflation over time, preserving the purchasing power of your investment income.

Strategies for Building Generational Wealth with Dividend Stocks

To maximize the benefits of dividend stocks and create a legacy of prosperity, consider the following strategies:

1. **Choose Blue-Chip Companies:** Focus on established, industry-leading companies with a track record of reliable dividend payments. These "blue-chip" stocks often provide stability and consistent returns over the long term. Think Coca Cola (KO), Johnson & Johnson (JNJ), Target (TGT), Walmart (WMT), etc.

2. **Embrace Dividend Growth Investing ("DGI"):** Prioritize companies that not only pay dividends but also have a history of increasing them annually. This strategy ensures that your investment income keeps pace with inflation and grows over time. Think Coca Cola (KO), IBM (IBM), Caterpillar (CAT), Exxon-Mobile (XOM), McDonald's (MCD), Proctor & Gamble (PG), etc.

3. **Diversify Your Portfolio:** Spread your investments across multiple sectors and industries to mitigate risk and capture opportunities for growth. Diversification is key to building a resilient investment portfolio that can weather market fluctuations. Think the information technology, real estate, consumer staples, materials financial, and healthcare sectors.

4. **Adopt a Long-Term Mindset:** Building generational wealth requires patience and discipline. Stay committed to your investment plan, even during periods of market volatility, and resist the temptation to engage in short-term speculation.

Harnessing Cumulative Dividends for Lasting Wealth

Cumulative dividends play a crucial role in preserving and enhancing the wealth-building potential of dividend stocks. By reinvesting missed dividend payments, investors can compound their returns over time, ensuring a steady stream of income and long-term growth. Additionally, understanding the tax implications of dividend investing can help investors minimize tax liabilities and maximize after-tax returns.

Empowering Future Generations Through Financial Education

Passing on wealth requires more than just financial resources; it requires knowledge and education. Take the time to teach your children and grandchildren about the value of money, the principles of investing, and the importance of long-term financial planning. By instilling these lessons early on, you empower future generations to continue the legacy of prosperity you've established.

Nurturing a Legacy of Prosperity

In conclusion, dividend stocks represent a powerful tool for building and preserving generational wealth. By strategically investing in dividend-paying companies, reinvesting dividends, and educating future generations, you can create a legacy of prosperity that extends far beyond your lifetime. With diligence, patience, and a long-term perspective, you can sow the seeds of financial abundance today and reap the rewards for generations to come.

CHAPTER 6:
Maximizing Generational Wealth with High-Yield Savings Accounts

"Make a quick switch from a traditional savings account to a high-yield savings account."

—**Vivian Tu**, *Quotes From Financial Gurus: The Smartest Ways To Use Your Savings*

IN THE PURSUIT of building and safeguarding generational wealth, high-yield savings accounts emerge as a powerful tool, offering a pathway to financial security and prosperity. In this chapter, we'll explore the dynamics of high-yield savings accounts, their advantages, considerations, and their pivotal role in shaping a legacy of abundance for future generations.

Understanding High-Yield Savings Accounts: Unleashing Financial Potential

High-yield savings accounts represent a significant departure from traditional savings vehicles, offering higher interest rates and accelerated growth potential for your hard-earned money. But what sets them apart, and how can they contribute to the creation of generational wealth?

What Sets High-Yield Savings Accounts Apart?

At their core, high-yield savings accounts function similarly to regular savings accounts but with one crucial distinction: they offer substantially higher interest rates. This means that for every dollar you deposit, you earn a more substantial return over time compared to traditional savings accounts. Think about where you keep your money now. Maybe it's in a regular savings account, which might give you something like 0.50% interest. But with a high-yield savings account, you could get a rate as high as 5.00%. Let's do the math: If you put $10,000 in a regular savings account, you'd have around $10,050 after a year. But with a high-yield savings account, you'd have about $10,500. That's a big difference!

The Magic of Compound Interest

The magic of high-yield savings accounts lies in the concept of compound interest. Remember, the key to creating wealth is not just about saving money; it's about making your money work for you. As your money earns interest, those earnings are reinvested, generating additional interest. Over time, this compounding effect snowballs, resulting in accelerated growth of your savings.

Advantages and Disadvantages of High-Yield Savings Accounts

Before diving into high-yield savings, it's essential to weigh the pros and cons:

Advantages:

- **Higher Interest Rates:** High-yield savings accounts offer significantly higher interest rates compared to traditional savings accounts, maximizing your earning potential.
- **Easy Access to Funds:** Unlike long-term investments, funds in high-yield savings accounts are easily accessible, providing liquidity and flexibility for short-term financial goals.
- **Safety:** High-yield savings accounts are FDIC-insured up to a certain limit, ensuring the safety of your deposits.

Disadvantages:

- **Rate Fluctuations:** Interest rates on high-yield savings accounts are subject to change, potentially impacting your earnings over time.
- **Limited Physical Branches:** Many high-yield savings accounts are offered by online banks, meaning there may not be physical branches for in-person banking.

- **Minimum Balance Requirements:** Some high-yield savings accounts may require a minimum balance to maintain the high-interest rate, imposing constraints on account holders.

Strategic Considerations for High-Yield Savings Accounts

High-yield savings accounts are particularly well-suited for certain financial goals and scenarios:

- **Short-Term Savings Goals:** If you're saving for short-term objectives like a vacation, emergency fund, or down payment on a home, high-yield savings accounts offer a safe and lucrative option.
- **Capital Preservation:** High-yield savings accounts provide a balance between safety and growth, making them ideal for individuals seeking to preserve capital while earning a competitive return.
- **Wealth Accumulation:** By consistently contributing to a high-yield savings account, you can harness the power of compound interest to build substantial wealth over time.

Empowering Future Generations

One of the most compelling aspects of high-yield savings accounts is their potential to empower future generations. By establishing and nurturing a high-yield savings account, you lay the groundwork for a legacy of financial abundance that can benefit your children, grandchildren, and beyond.

Building a Legacy of Prosperity

In conclusion, high-yield savings accounts serve as a cornerstone in the construction of generational wealth, offering a blend of safety, growth, and accessibility. By leveraging the power of compound interest and strategic financial planning, you can unlock new avenues for prosperity and secure a brighter future for yourself and your loved ones. So, seize the opportunity today, and embark on a journey towards lasting financial security and abundance.

CHAPTER 7:
Safeguarding Your Wealth: Strategies to Shield Against Financial Erosion

"Preserving and protecting financial wealth requires an understanding of, and a solid plan for, counteracting the three primary forces that erode wealth over multiple generations. Just as water, wind, and gravity work to erode national monuments, three forces work to erode financial wealth over multiple generations."

Garrett B Gunderson, *What Would the Rockefellers Do?: How the Wealthy Get and Stay That Way, and How You Can Too*

I N THE PURSUIT of generational wealth, protecting assets from erosion caused by banks and taxes is paramount. Just as monumental structures withstand the forces of nature through strategic defense, your financial wealth requires a robust shield against the erosive influences of division, taxation, and external risks. Let me break it down for you in simple terms. Consider your wealth as a precious treasure, susceptible to erosion if left unprotected. Just like water, wind, and gravity wear down mighty monuments, there are three things that can chip away at your financial wealth over time:

1. **Splitting Up Your Money:** When wealth gets divided among different generations, it can shrink over time. Imagine splitting a pie into smaller and smaller pieces. Managing the transfer of assets across generations is crucial to preserving wealth over time. To keep your money strong, you need to have a plan to make sure it stays together.

2. **Taxation:** Transfer and capital gain taxes can nibble away at your wealth. It's like paying tolls every time you want to use your money. Mitigating tax liabilities through strategic planning is essential for minimizing taxes and keeping more of your money in your pocket.

3. **Safeguarding Against Risks:** Just as a fortress requires protection from external threats, your wealth demands defenses against business risks and potential attacks. Establishing robust safeguards is vital to shield your assets from harm and ensure their enduring security.

To safeguard your wealth from these threats, meticulous planning and strategic utilization of financial instruments are indispensable. By implementing effective strategies, you can fortify your financial fortress and secure the longevity of your wealth for future generations. To keep your money together, you need to take some time and think ahead about specific instructions you will need to include in a will and trust. We will cover more on these instruments in Chapter 11. Understanding key tax codes and leveraging tax-deferred vehicles are critical components of wealth preservation and growth. Among other things, to shield their money from banks and taxes the wealthy use the two powerful instruments known as Roth Individual Retirement Accounts ("IRA") and 7702 Plans. With Roth IRAs and 7702 plans, you can protect your wealth and keep more of your money away from pesky taxes. They're like secret weapons to secure your wealth and make sure you keep more of what you earn. It's like building a fortress around your hard-earned cash. Finally, forming and conducting business under a strategically created entity such as a trust is another example of how the wealthy shield their wealth from business risks and external threats. In this chapter we will focus on strategies to avoid transfer and capital gain taxes nibbling at your wealth by using tax-deferred financial instruments like ROTH IRAs and 7702 Plans and how the wealthy do it.

Roth IRAs: Harnessing Tax-Free Growth Potential

Roth IRAs offer a potent avenue for tax-free growth and preservation of wealth. By contributing after-tax dollars to a Roth IRA, you unlock the potential for tax-free growth and withdrawals in retirement. This tax-free status extends to both contributions and earnings, providing a compelling incentive for long-term wealth accumulation.

Strategic utilization of Roth IRAs is particularly advantageous for individuals anticipating higher tax brackets in retirement or seeking to diversify their tax exposure. By harnessing the tax-free growth potential of Roth IRAs, you can shield your wealth from the erosive effects of taxation and secure a stable financial future for yourself and your heirs.

Navigating the Regulatory Landscape: Strategic Insights into 72(t) Provisions

Internal Revenue Code ("IRC") section 72(t) provides a valuable avenue for accessing assets in IRAs and employer-sponsored retirement plans. For Fortune 500 employees with certain conditions, they offer penalty-free access under specific circumstances such as death, disability, first-time home purchases, and substantially equal periodic payments. While traditional retirement accounts typically impose a 10% penalty on early withdrawals, section 72(t) exemptions provide avenues for accessing funds before retirement age without incurring this penalty. Whether for emergency financial needs or strategic retirement planning, this rule offers crucial flexibility and liquidity for wealth preservation and financial stability.

Leveraging IRC Section 72(t) for Financial Flexibility

Understanding the nuances of 72(t) payments, including payment duration, frequency, calculation methods, and penalty avoidance strategies is essential for maximizing its benefits and optimizing retirement planning strategies:

- **Early Withdrawal Exemptions:** While traditional

withdrawals incur a 10% penalty, 72(t) payments offer exceptions for qualifying circumstances.

- **Payment Schedule Considerations:** Establishing a consistent payment schedule is vital, with options such as the required minimum distribution method, fixed amortization method, and fixed annuitization method.

- **Penalty Avoidance:** Modifying payment schedules prematurely can trigger penalties and interest retro-actively, emphasizing the importance of adherence to established terms.

- **Recent Changes and Opportunities:** Notice 2022-6 from the IRS introduces favorable changes, allowing for higher interest rates in 72(t) calculations, thereby enhancing potential distributions and optimizing retirement planning strategies.

7702 Plans: Maximizing Tax Advantages in Life Insurance

Section 7702 of the IRC delineates the guidelines for tax-advantaged life insurance policies, known as "7702 Plans". These plans encompass various cash value life insurance policies, including whole, universal, variable, or indexed policies, offering a tax-advantaged framework for wealth preservation. Contrary to its name, it's not a stand-alone plan but rather a category encompassing various cash value life insurance policies, including whole, universal, variable, or indexed policies. They're like super-powered life insurance policies that keep your money safe from taxes.

Similar to Roth IRAs, contributions to 7702 Plans accumulate on a tax-deferred basis, enabling potential long-term growth without immediate tax implications. Additionally, withdrawals from 7702 Plans are typically tax-free, providing liquidity for retirement needs without incurring tax liabilities. Moreover, the death benefit remains tax-free, ensuring financial security for beneficiaries and perpetuating wealth across generations.

TEFRA, DEFRA, TAMRA: Legislative Cornerstones of Wealth Preservation

The Tax Equity and Fiscal Responsibility Act ("TEFRA"), the Deficit Reduction Act ("DEFRA"), the Technical and Miscellaneous Revenue Act ("TAMRA"), along with Section 7702 of the IRC, constitute foundational elements of legislation governing life insurance policies and tax-deferred growth. The tax advantages provided by TEFRA, DEFRA, and TAMRA assist to create a favorable environment for building and protecting wealth over time. Understanding the implications of these legislative acts is paramount for optimizing wealth preservation strategies and maximizing tax advantages.

TEFRA, enacted in 1982, establishes the framework for tax-deferred growth within life insurance policies, enabling policyholders to benefit from the compounding of investments without immediate tax consequences. Building on the principles of TEFRA, DEFRA, enacted in 1984, emphasizes efficient premium payments and ensures policyholders maintain eligibility for favorable tax treatment.

TAMRA, introduced in 1988, sustains tax benefits for life insurance policyholders by maintaining the tax-deferred status of policy growth. By upholding the provisions established by TEFRA and DEFRA, TAMRA safeguards the long-term viability of tax-advantaged life insurance policies, thereby facilitating wealth preservation and intergenerational wealth transfer.

Strategic Utilization of 7702 Plans for Financial Flexibility

7702 Plans offer the following avenues for strategic financial planning:

- **Tax-Deferred Growth:** Contributions to 7702 Plans accumulate on a tax-deferred basis, allowing for potential long-term growth without immediate tax implications.
- **Tax-Free Access to Cash Value:** Withdrawals from 7702 Plans are typically tax-free, providing liquidity for retirement purposes without incurring tax liabilities.
- **Death Benefit:** The death benefit remains tax-free, offering financial security for beneficiaries in the event of the insured's passing.
- **Distinguishing from Retirement Plans:** While 7702 Plans share similarities with retirement accounts, such as tax advantages, they differ in structure and investment focus.

Understanding these distinctions is crucial for informed decision-making.

Empowering Informed Decision-Making: Securing Your Financial Future

Preserving and protecting your financial wealth demands a comprehensive understanding of key tax codes, diligence, discipline, strategic planning, and proactive risk management. So, embark on this journey with confidence, armed with knowledge and fortified with strategic planning, and safeguard your wealth from banks, taxes, and other threats with unwavering resolve. By harnessing the power of tax-deferred vehicles such as Roth IRAs and 7702 Plans, navigating legislative frameworks, and leveraging expert insights, with diligence, discipline and a commitment to financial empowerment, you can protect your wealth from erosion and ensure a legacy of prosperity that withstands the test of time for generations to come.

CHAPTER 8:
Maximizing Wealth Protection with Life Insurance Strategies

"If there is anyone dependent on your income – parents, children, relatives – you need life insurance."

—Suze Orman

WELCOME TO CHAPTER 8 of our journey toward financial empowerment and generational wealth. As promised, let's talk about something super important that can set you and your family up for success: insurance. While the topic may seem mundane at first glance, its significance cannot be overstated. So, what's insurance all about? Life insurance serves as a safety net, shielding your family from unforeseen financial hardships in the event of your passing. But beyond mere protection, strategic utilization of life insurance can pave the way for long-term wealth accumulation and preservation. If something happens, insurance steps in to help you out financially. Life insurance pays death benefits and creates an instant estate, regardless of when death occurs. In this chapter, we will focus on exploring the various types of life insurance policies, their intricacies, and how they can create, grow, and preserve generational wealth and secure your family a prosperous financial future.

The Rockefellers' Blueprint: Lessons in Wealth Growth and Preservation

Have you ever wondered why some families seem to have it all, every generation? Well, it's about more than just having money—it's about knowing how to grow and protect it. Let's explore how the Rockefellers built their fortune using insurance to avoid the financial institutional agenda. You've heard of the Rockefellers, right? The Rockefellers stand as paragons of generational wealth, their legacy etched in the annals of history. What was their secret sauce? Among their myriad financial strategies, one cornerstone stands out: insurance.

Imagine life insurance not merely as a safeguard for the present, but as a beacon of hope for future generations. You get life insurance—a policy that pays out when you pass away. But here's the twist: You don't just get it for yourself. You get it for your kids, and they get it for their kids, and so on. Each generation adds to the policy, and when someone passes, the payout goes to the family. Now, think about it. Over time, as the family grows and more policies pile up, the payouts get bigger and bigger. It's like planting seeds of wealth that keep multiplying, ensuring your family's future for years to come.

The Rockefellers understood this principle implicitly, leveraging insurance policies to nurture their wealth across generations. With each passing of the torch, the flame of prosperity grew brighter, fueled by the cumulative compounding power of these policies. Remember, compounding is the concept of your money making money on its own. Generational wealth starts with your money making money for you and future generations. In other words, generational wealth allows the power of compounding to continue past your lifetime. Some consider compounding the 8th wonder of the world. But compounding goes beyond money; it also pertains to relationships and education. Everything we learn compounds into something new. In most scenarios, the power of compounding dies with the owner. However, when we introduce generational wealth, we can continue the process of compounding throughout multiple generations.

That's why it's vital to educate yourself about finances and make savvy choices for your future. So, there you have it. Wealth isn't just a dream—it's within your reach with the right knowledge. Don't fall for flashy promises or schemes. Take a cue from the Rockefellers and use insurance to build generational wealth for your family. Focus on building a strong foundation of wealth that lasts. And remember, stay sharp when dealing with financial institutions—your future is at stake!

The concept of insurance, in generic terms, may be defined as the transfer of risk from one party to another through a legal contract called a policy. A "policy" is a written contract in which one party promises to indemnify another against loss that arises from an unknown event. Ordinary life insurance is life insurance of commercial companies not issued on the weekly premium basis. Ordinary life insurance is the principal type of life insurance purchased in the United States and includes both temporary (term) life insurance, permanent (whole, universal, and variable) life insurance coverage, as well as endowment policies.

Term Life Insurance: Your Foundation for Financial Security

Term life insurance stands as the bedrock of financial security, offering robust coverage at an affordable price point. Unlike its permanent counterpart, term life insurance provides protection for a predetermined period, typically ranging from 5 to 30 years. The defining characteristic of term life insurance lies in its simplicity and cost-effectiveness. By paying fixed premiums, policyholders secure a death benefit that safeguards their loved ones' financial well-being in the event of premature death. Term life is the CHEAPEST type of pure life insurance, and due to having a termination date and not having any cash value, it will ALWAYS be cheaper than a whole life policy with the same face value.

Key Variants of Term Life Insurance:

1. Level Term Insurance: Under this arrangement, policyholders pay consistent premiums in exchange for a fixed death benefit throughout the policy term. Level term insurance offers predictability and stability, making it an ideal choice for those seeking reliable coverage.

2. Increasing Term Insurance: This variant entails a death benefit that grows incrementally over time, catering to evolving financial needs. The amount of increase is usually stated as specific amounts or as a percentage of the original amount. It may also be tied to a cost-of-living index, such as the Consumer Price Index. Increasing term insurance may be sold as a separate policy but is usually purchased as part of a package or a cost-of-living rider to a policy. With increasing term insurance, policyholders can align their coverage with anticipated future expenses, ensuring comprehensive protection for their families.

3. Decreasing Term Insurance: A decreasing term policy is a type of life policy which has a death benefit that adjusts periodically (according to a schedule) and is written for a specific period of time. As policyholders gradually pay off debts, the coverage diminishes accordingly, reflecting the diminishing financial obligations.

4. Convertible Term Life Insurance: Recognizing the fluid nature of financial circumstances, convertible term life insurance grants policyholders the flexibility to convert their temporary protection into permanent coverage without undergoing medical underwriting. The option to convert must be included in the contract when the policy is purchased and depending on the insurance company, may specify a time limit for converting, such as 3 years prior to expiration or before age 55. Policies containing the option to convert are named accordingly and are easy to identify. For example, a term policy that provides life insurance protection for 15 years and also has a "conversion privilege" is called a 15-year convertible term policy. The option to convert gives the insured the right to convert or exchange the term policy for a whole life (or permanent) policy without evidence of insurability. This provision empowers individuals to adapt their insurance strategies in line with changing needs and aspirations.

5. Renewable Term Life Insurance: Offering continuity beyond the initial policy term, renewable term life insurance enables policyholders to extend coverage without proving insurability. Like the option to convert, the option to renew must be included in the contract when the policy is purchased. The premiums for the renewal period will be higher than the initial period, reflecting the insured's increased age and the insurer's increased risk. This steady increase in premium is often called a "step-up premium;" as you renew the policy, you climb up another "step." For example, if you have a 10-year renewable and convertible term; after the 10 years are up, the policy terminates, or you can renew it. If you renew it, the premium price will go up, and you will have the policy for another 10 years. This cycle continues until you are too old to renew or it's too expensive. As the premiums increase each renewal, the cost of the policy typically becomes cost prohibitive, forcing those who are older, and more likely to need the protection, to terminate or not renew the coverage. Annually renewable term or yearly renewable term provides coverage for one year and allows the policyowner to renew coverage each year, without evidence of insurability. This represents the most basic form of life insurance. This renewal is typically automatic and renews at an increased premium. This type of policy provides you with two sets of premium rates: a current or scheduled premium and a guaranteed maximum premium. While premiums may escalate with each renewal, this option ensures uninterrupted protection, irrespective of evolving health conditions.

Key Takeaways

Term life insurance can be a smart move for building wealth in some scenarios because it's way cheaper than other types of insurance, so you can get a lot of coverage for a small monthly payment. Plus, if you invest the money you save by choosing term insurance, it can really add up over time. But here's the thing to remember: ALL TERM insurance has a FINAL TERMINATION date where you can no longer renew it. Once that time is up, you're no longer covered. So, it's important to think about your family's long-term needs and make sure you have a plan in place for when your policy expires.

Advantages of term life insurance include:

- it is less expensive than permanent insurance;
- it may protect the insured's insurability if renewable and or convertible;
- it may be used in conjunction with debts, mortgages, or as a supplement to whole life insurance; and
- it provides the greatest amount of protection for the lowest cost.

Disadvantages of term life insurance include:

- that no protection is in effect once the term protection ends;
- if renewable or convertible, premium rates rise as the insured ages;
- due to the temporary nature of term insurance, few

death claims are actually paid under term insurance policies; and

- it possesses no equity (*i.e.*, cash value). Since it has no cash value, it does not mature as does a whole life policy.

Unlocking Generational Wealth with Whole Life Insurance: Building Wealth and Security for a Lifetime

Now, there's this thing called whole life insurance, and it's pretty cool. It's not just about covering you in case something happens (like traditional insurance does), but it's also an investment in your future. Where term life is designed to provide temporary protection for IF the insured dies too soon, whole life insurance is designed to provide permanent protection for WHEN the insured dies. This form of life insurance policy never needs to be converted or renewed, since it remains in force as long as all premiums are paid in a timely fashion. Whole life is often compared to BUYING; like BUYING a house. That money can help cover things like funeral costs, bills, or even leave something behind for your kids or grandkids.

Plus, it builds up cash value over time, kind of like a savings account. The cash value that builds up over time? You can actually borrow against it or even withdraw some of it if you need cash down the road. Just remember, if you dip into it early, there might be some penalties. Oh, and here's another cool thing: The money in your whole life policy grows tax-deferred. That means you don't have to pay taxes on it until you actually take it out. And if you're strategic about it, you can minimize those taxes even more.

Whole life insurance provides death benefits for the entire life of the insured. It also provides living benefits in the form of cash values. Whole life policies are based upon the assumption that premiums will be paid by the policyowner throughout the insured's lifetime or to age 100, whichever occurs first. This means that the whole life policy is designed to "mature" or "endow" at age 100. "Mature" or "endow" means that the cash value accumulations are equal to the face amount. The cash value and endowment (or maturity) are the main features distinguishing whole life insurance from term life insurance and combine to produce additional living benefits for the policyowner. All whole life lasts until death or age 100, has a fixed premium, and level benefit with cash value accumulation, regardless of how it is paid. Accordingly, the amount of premium for a whole life policy is calculated, in part, on the basis of the number of years between the insured's age at issue and age 100. The shorter the payment period, the higher the premium. This time span represents the full premium-paying period, with the amount of the premium spread equally over that period. This is known as the level premium approach. As is also the case with level premium term insurance, this approach allows whole life insurance premiums to remain level rather than increase each year with the insured's age.

The amount of a policy's cash value depends on a variety of factors, including:

- The face amount of the policy;
- The larger the face amount of the policy, the larger the cash values;

- The duration and amount of the premium payments;
- The shorter the premium-payment period, the quicker the cash values grow;
- The higher the premium amount, the quicker the cash values grow;
- How long the policy has been in force; and
- The longer the policy has been in force, the greater the build-up in cash values.

While all whole life insurance policies have the same type of benefits, there are different types of whole life insurance. Whole life insurance policies may also be referred to as straight life, continuous premium life, permanent life insurance or ordinary life. The only difference in "types" of whole life is how the policy is paid. There's the straight-up, pay-until-you-die kind, where you pay premiums for your entire life and coverage lasts as long as you do. Then there's limited pay, where you pay premiums for a set number of years, but coverage lasts your whole life. And hey, there's even a modified version where you get a break on premiums for the first few years. Some will be paid straight until death or age 100, some will be paid for after a few years or by a specific age, some may give you a little discount in the early years to help you get started, etc. Practically speaking, very few people live to age 100. It's far more likely that a whole life policy will be cashed in for its surrender value or that its face amount will be paid out as a death benefit prior to maturity.

By amalgamating insurance protection with a cash value accumulation mechanism, whole life insurance transcends mere risk mitigation, serving as a vehicle for wealth accumulation and intergenerational asset transfer.

Key Attributes of Whole Life Insurance:

1. **Permanent Protection:** Whole life insurance guarantees lifelong coverage, ensuring that beneficiaries receive a death benefit regardless of when the insured passes away. This permanence confers peace of mind and enduring financial security to policyholders and their families.

2. **Cash Value Accumulation:** A distinguishing feature of whole life insurance lies in its cash value component, which accrues over time. Similar to a savings account, the cash value serves as a reservoir of wealth that policyholders can access through loans or withdrawals, offering liquidity and financial flexibility.

3. **Premium Stability:** With whole life insurance, premiums remain fixed throughout the policy's duration, shielding policyholders from unexpected cost escalations. This predictability facilitates long-term financial planning and eliminates the uncertainty associated with fluctuating premiums.

4. **Variants of Whole Life Insurance:** Whole life insurance encompasses various iterations tailored to diverse financial needs and preferences. From traditional whole life policies to limited pay and modified options, individuals can select the structure that aligns with their unique circumstances and objectives.

Whole Life – Limited Pay

With Whole Life - Limited Pay the coverage remains on a limited-pay life policy until age 100 or death, whichever happens first. Even though the premium payments are limited to a certain period, the insurance protection extends until the insured's death, or to age 100. For example, if you were to purchase a 20-pay policy, premiums would need to be paid for 20 consecutive years. After that, you would not be required to make any additional premium payments, and your coverage would be guaranteed until death or age 100. A 40-year-old applicant who would like to retire at age 70 and wants a policy with level premiums, permanent protection, and premiums paid up at retirement would also choose a paid-up-at age-70 limited pay policy. A limited pay life insurance policy covers an insured's whole life with level premiums paid over a limited time.

Whole Life – Modified

Whole Life - Modified is a policy where the premium stays fixed for the first 5 years, and then increases in year 6 and stays level for the remainder of the policy. Modified whole life has all of the same features of any other whole life except the insurance company cuts you a break on premium for the first few years. Modified Whole Life describes a whole life policy with a premium that increases once after the first few years and then remains level for the remainder of the policy.

Whole Life – Modified Endowment Contract

Whole Life - Modified Endowment Contract ("MEC") is best described as a policy that exceeds the maximum amount of premium that can be paid into a policy or "overfunded" and still have it recognized as a life insurance contract. A policy that is overfunded, according to IRS tables, is classified as a MEC because it does not meet the 7-pay test. For that reason, the policy will lose favorable tax treatment. The 7-pay test is a limitation on the total amount you can pay into your policy in the first seven years of its existence. The test is designed to discourage premium schedules that would result in a paid-up policy before the end of a seven-year period. For example, if your annual premium for a policy was $1,000 and you paid $20,000 in the first five years, you will have failed the 7-pay test by exceeding $7,000 (7- years times one year of premium). Said differently, you have exceeded the maximum amount of premium that can be paid into a policy and still have it recognized as a life insurance contract. Some of the key implications associated with MECs are:

- If withdrawn prior to age 59 1/2, there is a 10% penalty.
- Taxation only occurs when cash is distributed.
- Funds withdrawn from a MEC are subject to last-in first-out ("LIFO") tax treatment, which assumes that the investment or earnings portion of the contract's values is withdrawn first (making these funds fully taxable as ordinary income).
- Penalty taxes on premature distributions from a MEC normally apply to policy loans.

Advantages of whole life insurance include:

- You're guaranteed to get death benefits.
- Your premiums stay the same, no surprises.
- You can pay off the policy early if you want.
- Need cash later on? You can borrow against your policy.
- Sometimes, the interest and cash payouts are tax-free.

Disadvantages of whole life insurance include:

- The interest rate might not always be great.
- You might miss out on higher returns.
- You have to keep paying your premiums consistently.

Indexed Universal Life Insurance: Balancing Growth Potential with Stability

Indexed universal life ("IUL") insurance represents a dynamic fusion of insurance protection and investment growth potential. IULs are the newer, more flexible option. It's a way to potentially earn interest based on market performance while still enjoying the security of a life insurance policy. The cash value grows based on the performance of an underlying index, such as the S&P 500. The policyholder can choose from a variety of indexes. IUL insurance policies typically contain a minimum guaranteed fixed interest rate component along with the indexed account option. Indexed policies give policyholders the security of fixed universal life insurance with the growth potential of a variable policy linked to indexed returns. Since IULs are tied to the stock market there's potential for higher returns if the stock market does well and so they are considered to be more like a retirement savings plan. Whole life insurance is usually seen as the safer bet if you want something predictable. But if you're willing to take on a little more risk for the chance of bigger rewards, an IUL might be more your style. Like term and whole life insurance policies, there are different types of IULs.

Explaining Types of IULs

Here's a summary of the different types of IUL insurance policies:

1. **Fixed Interest IUL:** In this type of policy, the cash value portion earns interest based on the performance of a fixed interest rate declared by the insurance company. The rate is typically guaranteed not to fall below a certain minimum level.

2. **Indexed Interest IUL:** With this policy, the cash value accumulation is tied to the performance of a stock market index, such as the S&P 500. The insurance company credits interest based on the index's performance, subject to a cap rate and sometimes a participation rate. Caps limit the maximum interest credited, while participation rates determine what percentage of the index's gain is credited to the policy.

3. **Guaranteed Universal Life with Indexing Options:**

These policies offer a death benefit guaranteed to a certain age (*e.g.*, 90 or 100), with the cash value portion having indexing options similar to IUL policies. However, these policies focus more on the death benefit and less on cash value accumulation.

4. **Variable Universal Life with Indexing Options:** These policies combine the features of Variable Universal Life ("VUL") insurance with indexing options. Policyholders can allocate their premiums to different investment accounts (subaccounts) similar to mutual funds, while also having the option to link some or all of their cash value to indexed accounts.

5. **Policy Riders and Customization:** Many IUL policies offer various riders and customization options to tailor the policy to the policyholder's needs. These may include options for accelerated death benefits, long-term care benefits, premium flexibility, and more.

Understanding the different types of IUL insurance policies allows individuals to choose the one that best fits their financial goals, risk tolerance, and insurance needs. Consulting with a financial advisor or insurance professional can provide further guidance in selecting the most suitable policy.

Key Advantages of IUL Insurance:

1. **Death Benefit Protection:** Like other forms of life insurance, IUL policies furnish beneficiaries with a tax-free death benefit, ensuring financial security in the event of the insured's demise.

2. **Cash Value Market-Linked Growth:** IUL insurance enables policyholders to participate in market gains through indexed accounts, thereby capitalizing on the stock market's growth potential. This indexed approach provides a pathway to superior returns while mitigating downside risk.

3. **Tax-Advantaged Accumulation:** The cash value component of IUL policies grows on a tax-deferred basis, shielding policyholders from immediate tax liabilities and maximizing the accumulation of wealth over time. Importantly, you won't pay taxes on the growth until you withdraw it (if at all).

4. **Flexibility and Customization:** IUL policies afford policyholders flexibility in premium payments and investment strategies, empowering individuals to tailor their insurance solutions to suit their evolving financial goals and risk tolerance.

5. **Creditor Protection:** In many states, the cash value and death benefit of life insurance policies, including IULs, are protected from creditors.

Key Disadvantages of IUL Insurance:

1. **Complexity:** IUL policies can be complex, with various features and options that may be difficult to understand.
2. **Cost:** The cost of insurance and administrative fees associated with IUL policies can be higher compared to term life insurance or other investment options.
3. **Market Risk:** While the cash value has the potential to grow based on market performance, it's also subject to market downturns, which could result in lower returns or even losses.
4. **Caps and Floors:** Some IUL policies have caps and floors on the returns, limiting the upside potential during strong market periods and protecting against losses during downturns.
5. **Surrender Charges:** Surrender charges may apply if you withdraw funds from the cash value or surrender the policy in the early years, limiting liquidity.

Crafting Your Financial Legacy

In conclusion, life insurance stands as a cornerstone of financial planning, offering both protection and wealth-building opportunities. Whether opting for term life insurance's affordability, whole life insurance's permanence and cash value growth, or indexed universal life insurance's market-linked returns, individuals can leverage diverse insurance strategies to fortify their financial legacies. As

African Americans seeking to transcend historical disparities and secure intergenerational wealth, informed decision-making and strategic utilization of life insurance can pave the path to prosperity. Remember, there's a financial advisor who stands ready to guide you through this journey, helping you navigate the complexities and optimize your insurance strategies for maximum impact. Together, let us forge a future of financial empowerment and generational wealth for ourselves and our communities.

CHAPTER 9:
Exploring Advanced Insurance Strategies for Generational Wealth

"Fun is like life insurance; the older you get, the more it costs."

—Kim Hubbard

I N THIS CHAPTER, we delve into the intricate world of insurance beyond the conventional life policies we've discussed earlier. These advanced insurance instruments offer a nuanced approach to building and safeguarding generational wealth, catering to specific needs and aspirations. From joint policies to variable life insurance, each option serves as a strategic tool in your financial arsenal. In this chapter, we will focus on exploring the various types of life insurance policies, their intricacies, and advanced strategies on how they can be used to create, grow, and preserve your wealth and secure you and your loved one's a prosperous financial future.

1. Joint Life Policy: Building Together for the Future: Think of a joint life policy as a shared investment in the future, much like a joint checking account but for life insurance. This policy covers two individuals, and upon the death of one, the surviving partner receives the full benefit. By covering two lives under one policy, joint life insurance cleverly leverages the ages of both insured parties to save on premiums. It's a smart way to protect your loved ones while optimizing financial resources.

2. Joint Survivor or Last Survivor Life Policies: Ensuring Lasting Protection: This insurance vehicle ensures lasting protection for you and your partner. Similar to the joint life policy, a joint survivor or last survivor life policy averages the ages of both insured individuals for premium savings and covers two individuals, but the benefit is paid out only after the passing of the last insured person. This means that if you and your partner obtain this policy, the benefit won't be triggered until both of you are gone. It's a testament to long-term commitment and financial security for future generations.

3. Family Maintenance Policy: Providing Ongoing Support: Imagine a steady stream of support for your family even after you're gone. That's precisely what a family maintenance policy offers—a monthly income for a specified period, coupled with a lump sum payout at the end. It serves as a lifeline for your loved ones, providing stability and comfort during challenging times. With a family maintenance policy, you ensure that your family's financial needs are met even in your absence.

4. Family Income Policy: A Safety Net for Your Loved Ones: A family income policy acts as a financial safety net for your family, offering immediate income upon your passing and continuing for a predetermined duration. It provides peace of mind and stability during times of transition, ensuring that your loved ones are supported financially. By securing a family income policy, you demonstrate your commitment to safeguarding your family's financial future.

5. Adjustable Life Policy: Flexibility for Changing Needs: Flexibility is the hallmark of an adjustable life policy. Designed to adapt to your evolving financial needs, it allows you to adjust premiums and death benefits as circumstances change. An adjustable life policy owner is usually looking for a policy offering flexible premiums. Adjustable life policies are able to provide these features by combining whole life and term life into a single plan. If a policyowner was looking for a policy in which they could control the amount and frequency of payments with a death benefit that can be adjusted as their life needs change, they would want an adjustable life policy. There typically are no dividends involved with adjustable life policies. Increasing the face amount may require a policy-owner to provide proof of insurability. With an adjustable life policy, you have insurance that grows with you, ensuring that your coverage remains aligned with your life goals and priorities. Whether you need to increase or decrease your coverage, an adjustable life policy offers the flexibility you need to navigate life's uncertainties.

6. Term Rider: Cost-Effective Coverage for the Whole Family: A term rider is a cost-effective solution for covering your entire family under one policy. Typically attached to a main policy covering the family head, term riders provide level term coverage for the spouse and children. A term rider is always level term. This is cheaper than every family member getting their own policy. For example, the main policy may be on dad, then mom and the children are riding on (attached to) dad's policy as term riders. Term riders allow for additional family members to be covered under one policy by attaching everyone to a main policy. Term riders can also allow an applicant to have excess coverage by adding an additional term rider for them to the main policy. By consolidating coverage under a single policy, you save on premiums while ensuring that your family is protected financially.

Through an understanding and strategic use of these advanced insurance instruments, you can create a robust financial foundation for yourself and your loved ones. By carefully selecting the policies that align with your goals and aspirations, you set the stage for long-term prosperity and generational wealth.

Variable Life Insurance Policies: Navigating Market Volatility

Variable life insurance policies offer a unique approach to insurance by incorporating investment components. Variable life insurance policies let you invest part of your premium in stocks, bonds, or mutual funds. Also known as interest-sensitive policies, these policies have a fixed level premium, and the death benefit is guaranteed, but the cash value can fluctuate based on the performance of the underlying investment portfolio. Your death benefit can also increase if the earnings of that separate fund increase. Variable life insurance products do not make any promises as to guaranteed cash values, interest rates, or minimum cash values so it's the policyowner who assumes the investment risk. What these products do offer is the potential to realize investment gains that exceed those available with traditional life insurance policies. This is done by allowing policyowners to direct the investment of the funds that back their variable contracts through separate account options.

By placing their policy values into separate accounts, policyowners can participate directly in the account's investment performance, which will earn a variable (as opposed to a fixed) return. Functioning on much the same principle as mutual funds, the return enjoyed-by or loss suffered-by policyowners through their investment in a separate account is directly related to the performance of the assets underlying the separate account. Separate accounts are not insured by the insurer and the returns on their investments are not guaranteed. For the insurer, this presents a means of transferring the investment risk from itself to the policyowner. The insurer can offer policyowners the possibility (though not the guarantee) of competitively high returns without facing the investment risk posed by its guaranteed fixed policies. This policy may be advantageous for a person who wishes to experience a potentially greater rate of return or degree of growth of the cash savings value. It also provides a policyowner with flexibility and control over the investment portion of the contract. It's like having insurance with a side of potential growth.

If a policyowner or applicant was looking for a policy to offset inflation, they would want to look into a variable policy. While variable life insurance policies offer the potential for higher returns, they also come with investment risk. Policyholders assume the risk associated with market fluctuations, and there are no guarantees regarding cash values or interest rates. Since the policyowner is assuming all of the investment risk and the rate of return is not guaranteed, variable insurance products are considered securities contracts as well as insurance contracts. Therefore, they fall under the regulatory arm of both state offices of insurance regulation and the Securities and Exchange Commission. To sell variable insurance products, an individual must hold a life insurance license and a Financial Industry Regulatory Authority registered representative's license.

Types of Variable Life Insurance Policies:

1. **Variable Life:** These policies allow you to invest part of your premium in stocks, bonds, or mutual funds. While the death benefit is guaranteed, the cash value can vary based on market performance.

2. **Universal Variable Life:** With universal variable life policies, you have control over the investment of cash values and premium payments. This allows for greater flexibility in managing your policy.

3. **Variable Whole Life:** Similar to variable life policies, variable whole life insurance offers investment options along with a guaranteed death benefit. It combines the benefits of whole life insurance with the potential for investment growth.

4. **Variable Annuity:** Variable annuities function similarly to other variable life insurance policies but are designed to provide a stream of income during

retirement. They offer the potential for investment growth while ensuring a steady income in retirement.

In summary, variable life insurance policies offer a unique blend of insurance and investment components, allowing policyholders to participate in the potential growth of their policy's cash value. Variable policies can be beneficial for offsetting inflation and providing long-term growth potential, but they require an understanding of investment risk and careful planning.

CHAPTER 10:
Leveraging Annuities for Long-term Wealth Growth

"Asset allocation, where to park your money and how to divide it up, is the single most important skill of a successful investor."

—**Anthony Robbins**, *MONEY Master the Game: 7 Simple Steps to Financial Freedom*

WELCOME TO THE world of annuities—a powerful tool for building and safeguarding generational wealth. While they may seem complex at first glance, annuities are like specialized savings plans designed to help you grow and manage your money over time. In this chapter, we'll explore how annuities work, the different types available, and how they can play a crucial role in creating, growing, and preserving generational wealth to secure a prosperous financial future for you and your loved ones.

Understanding Annuities: Building Blocks of Financial Security

Annuities function as contractual agreements with insurance companies, offering a unique way to generate income over a specified period, often extending to a lifetime. Think of them like tools to help you grow and manage your money over time, kind of like a special savings plan. They serve as a financial safety net, allowing your money to grow tax-deferred until you begin withdrawals. Let's delve into the two primary types of annuities.

Fixed Annuities: Consistency and Reliability

Fixed annuities provide a stable and predictable option for wealth accumulation. These annuities guarantee a minimum interest rate for the duration of the contract, offering a safety net for your finances. With fixed annuities, you can avoid the volatility of the stock market while still enjoying steady growth on your investment.

Variable Annuities: Exploring Growth Opportunities

Variable annuities, on the other hand, offer a more dynamic approach to wealth management. As previously discussed, with variable annuities, you have the opportunity to invest your money in various options, akin to stocks or bonds. While this presents the potential for higher returns, it also comes with increased risk, as the performance of your investment is tied to market fluctuations.

Harnessing the Power of Stretch Annuities

One of the most compelling features of annuities, especially for building generational wealth, is the concept of stretch annuities. These specialized annuities enable you to pass on wealth to future generations while minimizing tax implications. Here's how it works:

- You contribute funds to a stretch annuity, where they grow tax-deferred over time.
- When you pass on the annuity to your children, they inherit the tax-deferred status, allowing the funds to continue growing without immediate tax consequences.
- Even your grandchildren can benefit from the stretch annuity, enjoying tax-deferred growth until they reach maturity.

Advantages Over Traditional Retirement Plans

While traditional retirement plans like 401(k)s and IRAs are valuable tools for retirement savings, annuities offer unique advantages, particularly in the realm of estate planning and wealth preservation. With a stretch annuity:

- You can minimize tax liabilities, allowing your wealth

to compound over generations without significant erosion from taxes.

- By gifting portions of the annuity to your children each year, you can avoid gift taxes while simultaneously transferring wealth.
- The income generated from the annuity can be used to purchase life insurance for your beneficiaries, further enhancing your estate plan.

Navigating Complexity with Professional Guidance

While annuities hold immense potential for long-term wealth growth, they require careful consideration and strategic planning. Consulting with a financial professional can help you navigate the complexities of annuities and tailor a strategy that aligns with your financial goals and aspirations. Whether you're aiming for a comfortable retirement or seeking to establish a legacy of prosperity for future generations, annuities can serve as a valuable tool in your financial arsenal.

In conclusion, annuities offer a pathway to financial security and prosperity, allowing you to grow and protect your wealth over time. By leveraging the unique features of annuities, such as stretch provisions, you can create a legacy of abundance for your family and future generations. With careful planning and professional guidance, you can unlock the full potential of annuities to build and safeguard generational wealth.

CHAPTER 11:
Preserving Your Wealth Through Pour Over Wills and Trusts

"The lesson is clear. If you want to empower your children, grandchildren and great-grandchildren, don't simply leave them money to spend as they please. Keep the money together. Design trusts that direct how money can and cannot be spent. And pass on your values to the next generation so that your vision doesn't stop with you."

—**Garrett B Gunderson**, *What Would the Rockefellers Do?: How the Wealthy Get and Stay That Way, and How You Can Too*

IN THE PURSUIT of generational wealth, ensuring the seamless transfer of assets across generations is paramount. One of the most significant threats to wealth accumulation is the division of assets among heirs, which can lead to the erosion of wealth over time. To combat this, integrating wills and trusts into your estate plan becomes crucial. Imagine a future where your hard-earned assets effortlessly transition to your loved ones, safeguarding their financial stability for generations. This future is not just a dream; it's a tangible reality within your grasp through the power of estate planning, where wills and trusts play pivotal roles. In this chapter, we will explore the importance of wills and trusts in estate planning that creates, grows and protects generational wealth to secure a prosperous financial future for you and your loved ones.

Advantages of a Will

A will serves as your voice beyond the grave, a legally binding document that dictates how your estate should be managed after your passing. With a will, you have the power to designate beneficiaries, distribute assets, appoint guardians for minor children, and specify funeral arrangements. Without a will, your estate could be subject to the decisions of a probate court, potentially leaving your loved ones without the provisions you intended. Regardless of your wealth status, everyone needs a will. It's not merely a formality but a strategic tool for minimizing tax liabilities and ensuring the seamless transition of assets to your chosen beneficiaries.

Key Notes on Wills

- A will is a legally binding document that dictates how your estate should be managed after your passing.
- You can designate beneficiaries, distribute assets,

appoint guardians for minor children, and specify funeral arrangements.

- Without a will, your estate could be subject to the decisions of a probate court, potentially leaving your loved ones without the provisions you intended.

Advantages of a Trust

A trust is a powerful tool for protecting and managing your assets for the benefit of your loved ones. It acts as a safety net, ensuring that your hard-earned money and property are used according to your wishes. There are primarily two types of trusts: testamentary trusts, which are created within a will and activated after your passing, and living trusts, which are established during your lifetime, providing flexibility and control. Within living trusts, there are two key variations: revocable living trusts, which offer flexibility, control, and privacy during your lifetime, and irrevocable living trusts, which provide asset protection and potential tax benefits by permanently transferring assets outside of your estate.

Key Notes on a Trust

- A trust is a powerful tool for protecting and managing your assets for the benefit of your loved ones.
- There are two main types of trusts: testamentary trusts and living trusts.
- A testamentary trust, also known as a will trust, is

a trust that's established in a person's last will and testament and goes into effect after their death. It's created to protect some or all of the deceased person's assets for the benefit of others.

- Living trusts offer flexibility, control, and privacy during your lifetime, while also ensuring a smooth transition of assets to your heirs after your passing.
- Irrevocable living trusts provide asset protection and potential tax benefits by permanently transferring assets outside of your estate.

Trust Statement of Purpose

The purpose of a trust is to safeguard your family's financial future, control and manage your assets effectively, simplify the distribution process, and potentially reduce taxes, saving your heirs a significant amount.

Funding a Trust

Funding a trust is essential for securing your assets for future generations. It involves transferring ownership of specific assets to the trustee of the trust, ranging from personal property like furniture and electronics to financial accounts and real estate. Understanding the process of funding a trust for different asset types ensures a smooth transition of ownership and management.

Asset Considerations

- **Real Property:** Transfer ownership to your trust to avoid probate and simplify future transfers.
- **Retirement Accounts:** While generally not funded into trusts, beneficiary designations can be updated to align with your estate plan.
- **Life Insurance:** Consider irrevocable trusts for tax advantages and greater control over distribution.
- **Personal Property:** Assign items like artwork and jewelry to your trust to ensure their seamless transfer.

Ongoing Management

Maintaining the integrity of your trust requires staying informed about major asset changes and regularly revisiting your estate plan, especially after significant life events. Professional guidance ensures that your trust remains effectively funded and aligned with your goals.

Tax Implications

Understanding the tax implications of trusts is crucial for minimizing tax burdens and maximizing benefits. Assets held in a grantor trust—a type of living trust-for example, are treated as if the trust creator still owns them for tax purposes, simplifying income tax reporting and financial management.

Key Takeaways

- Integrating wills and living trusts into your estate plan is crucial for preserving wealth and ensuring a seamless transfer of assets.
- A will dictates asset distribution, appoints guardians, and specifies funeral arrangements, while a trust protects and manages assets according to your wishes.
- Testamentary trusts and living trusts offer different benefits and variations, providing flexibility and control over asset distribution.
- Understanding tax implications is essential for minimizing tax burdens and maximizing benefits.
- Regularly revisiting your estate plan and seeking professional guidance ensures ongoing management and alignment with your goals.

FAQs

1. **Do I need a will?** Yes, a will is essential for dictating how your wealth will be handled and ensuring your wishes are carried out.
2. **Do I need a trust?** It depends on your assets and goals, but trusts can provide added control and protection for your estate.
3. **What's the difference between a trust and a will?** A will directs asset distribution through probate, while a trust bypasses probate and offers additional benefits.
4. **Will my assets avoid probate with a living trust?** Yes,

if properly funded, a living trust can help your assets bypass probate.

5. **How do I set up a living trust?** Consult with an attorney to create a customized plan that aligns with your goals and financial situation.

6. **Who should be trustees?** Trustees can include yourself, your spouse, or a combination of family members and professionals, depending on your preferences and circumstances.

Remember, estate planning is a proactive step towards securing your family's financial future. By establishing and funding a trust, you can protect your assets, minimize taxes, and ensure your legacy lives on for generations to come. With the right guidance and planning, you can create a robust estate plan that safeguards your wealth and provides peace of mind for you and your loved ones.

CHAPTER 12:
Crafting Your Financial Legacy: Strategies For Wealth Preservation

"For unto whomsoever much is given, of him shall be much required: and to whom men have committed much, of him they will ask the more."

—Luke 12:48 (KJV)

IN THE JOURNEY toward building and safeguarding generational wealth, the path is often as unique as the individuals embarking upon it. It's a journey marked by personal choices, informed decisions, and strategic planning. In this chapter, we will focus on practical strategies for crafting your financial legacy and drawing from real-life experiences and insights to empower you on your wealth-building journey.

My Personal Journey

I did not study economics, nor do I have an MBA. What I've always had was a desire to escape poverty and a desire to learn how to do so intelligently. I taught myself how to trade stocks by reading articles, watching YouTube videos, and practicing trading stocks on Google Finance back when I was in school between 2005-2008. After picking profitable stocks and watching my mock portfolio grow, I started to invest real money. It's a low bar but I knew I was successful because I started to build up my savings account and significantly lowered my debt.

I've always been a firm believer that I need to be a good steward because everything I have belongs to God and He expects me to be a good steward of what I've been entrusted with. With that said, when I turned 40, I seriously begin to contemplate what to do with the money I had been entrusted with. With children and my wife as a stay-at-home mom depending on my income, I knew I needed to start thinking strategically about how I would maintain their lifestyle if something happened to my income. No one likes to think about death, but the hard truth is that our spirit will leave our body one day, so we must accept the inevitable and prepare for it.

To start my journey, I started reading articles on estate planning and started gathering and organizing my financial information. In the process of getting my financial information together, a student I was teaching shared wealth management tips with me in hopes that I would select him to be my financial advisor. I sternly and passionately declined his invitation based on the logic that he was a broke college student, and I was a successful millionaire. The student understood my reasoning for declining the invitation but shared with me the book "*What Would the Rockefellers Do?: How the Wealthy Get and Stay That Way, and How You Can Too*" by Garret B. Gunderson. The book stayed untouched on my desk for three months until I decided to take it to read on an anniversary trip with my wife to St. Lucia. As I was reading the book, the detailed strategies that the wealthy use made a lot of sense and helped me organize my thoughts on what I could do with the IRAs and 401Ks that I was managing for my wife and myself. Most importantly, the book educated me on the importance of having insurance and how insurance could be used to fund my lifestyle while I am still alive. I've always known that I wanted to retire early so I formulated a strategy to allow me to enjoy my wealth while I was still healthy. So, after reading the book, I started writing down my short-term and long-term goals to be able to retire at 45.

Once I had this information, I reached out to my student who recommended the book and he paired me with a more experienced financial professional to assist me in strategically figuring out a way to build and protect my wealth for my family. Of course, I didn't just take his word for it! I read all types of articles on every step of the process. This is what made it easy for me to write this book. The financial advisor started his consultation by asking me questions about my current financial status and my goals for retirement. Because I was prepared and had done the research, I was able to email him all of this information. For your journey, I have compiled a list of what is needed at the end of the book to ensure your time with a financial advisor or professional is productive.

One of the key takeaways from my conversation with the financial professional was that I was blessed financially to be in a good position on my journey to creating, building and protecting my wealth. From the Rockefeller book, one of the things that stuck out to me was that the wealthy purposefully use financial institutions and use over-funded insurance policies as "Family Banks" for various strategic reasons. Over-funded insurance policies, such as IULs or Variable Universal Life insurance policies, allow policyholders to contribute premiums that exceed the amount required to maintain the death benefit. Instead of maximizing the death benefit, these policies focus on accumulating cash value, which grows tax-deferred. The excess premiums paid into the policy accumulate as cash value, which can be accessed through policy loans or withdrawals. Unlike traditional bank loans, policy loans do not require credit checks or approval from a financial institution, providing greater autonomy to the policyholder. Additionally, since policy loans are not subject to income tax, policyholders can access the cash-value tax-efficiently.

Families may use Family Banks by leveraging the accumulated cash value to finance various needs or opportunities. This can include funding educational expenses, purchasing real estate or other assets, providing liquidity for business ventures, or supplementing retirement income. Overall, Family Banks can serve as a valuable tool for families looking to create a source of tax-efficient liquidity and financial flexibility for various needs and opportunities. While Family Banks offer potential benefits, it's essential for families to carefully consider the associated risks, including policy fees, interest rates on policy loans, and the potential impact on the death benefit if loans are not repaid.

As previously discussed, whole life insurance policies are not cheap! Funding a Family Bank and other insurance policies would've been a financial strain if I decided to fund them from my monthly or annual income. However, I knew

I needed not only general insurance policies to benefit my family should something happen to me, but also to establish a Family Bank if I was serious about building generational wealth. For your benefit, I will briefly identify the steps I took to build and secure my family's wealth and establish a Family Bank for future generations.

Gather Your Financial Information

The foundation of any successful financial plan lies in a clear understanding of your current financial status. When you start the estate planning process it forces you to look at how efficient or wasteful you've been. Start by gathering and organizing your financial information, including assets, liabilities, investments, and expenses. Review your monthly and annual spending habits, scrutinizing both essential and discretionary expenses. How much is spent on luxury goods and vacations? How much is spent on bare necessities? This process provides invaluable insights into your financial health and lays the groundwork for informed decision-making.

Consider Your Long-Term and Short-Term Goals

As you embark on your wealth-building journey, it's essential to define your long-term objectives and short-term goals. Once you've got a good idea of your assets and liabilities as well as your basic monthly and annual expenses, you can determine the retirement income you desire and budget that is needed to continue to fuel your lifestyle. Educate yourself about financial planning principles and investment strategies, empowering yourself to make informed decisions about your financial future.

Create a Financial Plan

Armed with a clear understanding of your financial landscape and goals, it's time to create a comprehensive financial plan. Consult with a financial professional to develop a customized plan tailored to your unique circumstances, objectives, and goals. A well-crafted financial plan serves as a roadmap for wealth accumulation, preservation, and distribution, guiding your actions and decisions along the way.

Financial Advisor vs. Fiduciary

When seeking professional guidance, it's crucial to understand the difference between a financial advisor and a fiduciary. While both can offer valuable insights and advice, a fiduciary is legally obligated to act in your best interests, providing unbiased recommendations aligned with your goals. Choose a financial professional who operates as a fiduciary, ensuring that your interests remain paramount throughout the planning process.

My Personal Financial Plan

One of the objectives in my financial plan is that I want to retire at 45. To reach this objective, I transferred my investment funds sitting in IRAs and 401Ks (that I was self-managing) and eligible to be rolled over to purchase a 10-year fixed indexed annuity. Keep in mind that one part of financial institutions' agenda is to make it difficult to get your funds. This became evident in my journey. I will briefly address that learning experience later.

Although I was successful managing my investment accounts, I still carried the risk that I could lose my funds in a downturn or lose everything if the market crashed. By transferring these funds to an annuity, I allocated that risk to the annuity company. With the fixed indexed annuity, I had a choice to invests the funds in various indexes to gain compounding growth. I chose to allocate my funds evenly among two index strategies with an average annual return rate of 11.08%. In addition, the fixed indexed annuity I chose included an 18% bonus that applied as soon as I transferred my funds adding to my wealth.

The fixed indexed annuity will continue to provide the advantage of tax-deferred interest accumulation and I only pay taxes on the growth when I withdraw money. This interest is considered income and so I'm responsible for paying taxes on this income at the applicable rate. The fixed indexed annuity has an option for free annual withdrawals (up to 10% of the accumulated value) which are not subject to withdrawal charges so that works in my favor. Each year I can withdraw no less than $100K in interest without touching my principal (the amount I originally deposited) to fund whatever I want after paying taxes. I chose to use the income generated from the fixed indexed annuity (interest payment withdrawals) to purchase strategic life insurance policies to grow my wealth further.

At the fixed indexed annuity's mature date (10 years), I have the option to create a regular stream of income from my principal either for a certain period of time or for the rest of my life. After ten years, with this fixed indexed annuity, my annual withdrawals could equal no less than one million dollars solely off the interest while my principal continues to grow. My principal after ten years can be used as a death benefit which I can leave to my family further accomplishing my objectives in my financial plan.

Transfer Investment Funds to an Annuity

One strategy for safeguarding and growing your wealth is to transfer investment funds to an annuity. An annuity offers several benefits, including tax-deferred growth, guaranteed income options, and protection from market volatility. By allocating funds to an annuity, you can mitigate investment risk and secure a steady stream of income for retirement.

Be Wary of SOME Financial Institutions on Your Journey

My wife and I had several IRAs that were sitting with two different financial institutions - Fidelity and Merrill Edge. While we were easily able to complete and notarize an online form and send it in to get the funds transferred from Fidelity in a mere matter of days, we received the run-around from Merrill Edge (*e.g.*, went in-person to a bank, completed multiple forms, exchanged several calls and emails, etc.). Eventually, after weeks of persistence and paying over $500 we were able to secure a transfer of our funds.

While exploring investment options, it's essential to conduct thorough research and exercise caution. Be wary of investment platforms like Merrill Edge and carefully evaluate their offerings, fees, and reputation. Ask what you must do to secure and transfer your funds before you choose your financial institutions. Choose reputable and trustworthy investment providers that align with your financial goals and values.

My Personal Journey Continued

The next step after setting up the fixed indexed annuity was to establish a high yield savings account where the annual withdrawals could be automatically deposited and then withdrawn to pay for key insurance policies. Once the high yield savings account was established, I spoke with a financial professional about the best companies for various types of insurance policies. Again, I had already done my research and wanted to discern the credibility and intelligence of the financial professional.

I was determined to get a whole life insurance policy for myself, and I did my research on the best company to do so with. I'm not being paid by these companies so I'm not going to mention their name but it's easy to Google this information. The other type of policy I felt was needed was a family bank policy which could be properly over-funded (remember TAMRA, TEFRA and DEFRA?) and used as a bank by the family as our wealth grows. Any withdrawals or loans from the family bank are tax free. I also wanted IUL policies that could grow my wealth and be fully paid-up after 10 years for my wife and myself. Remember, IULs are insurance policies that grow the policy's value by investing in various indexes. In addition to the death benefit, my IULs are tied to the market and the value continues to grow over time with little risk to me since my policy has a floor.

Using the annuity, high yield savings account and IULs and other insurance policies I was able to ensure my money is making money for me while still maintaining the freedom of my current income. What does that mean? My current income can still be used on whatever I want to fund my family's lifestyle and I'm simultaneously building and securing wealth for my family behind the scenes!

The next step after setting up my insurance policies and automatic premium payment, was to execute a will and trust to ensure the money stays together, minimize tax implications and protect the money from outside risks. The will process was pretty straight forward, and I just needed to answer a few questions for the attorney to put it together. I have included some questions at the end of the book to help you get started. I completed a "pour-over will" which works in conjunction with a trust. It's called "pour over" because it directs any assets that haven't already been transferred to the trust during my lifetime to "pour over" into the trust upon my death. Essentially, it acts as a safety net to ensure that all my assets are eventually distributed according to the terms of my trust.

Trust Statement of Purpose

Establishing the trust is where I really had fun. One idea that I really liked from the Rockefeller book was that unlike Vanderbilt, he didn't leave his heirs money – he left them means and opportunity. A trust statement of purpose serves as a guiding document that outlines the intentions, objectives, and goals behind the establishment of a trust. I dedicated a lot of time to making sure that my trust statement of purpose laid out for the trustees and my future heirs the principles and values that I hold dear.

Here's why it's important:

1. **Clarity of Intentions:** A trust statement of purpose provides clarity regarding the creator's intentions for the trust assets. It articulates the specific goals and objectives that the trust is designed to achieve, such as providing for the care of beneficiaries, protecting assets, or supporting charitable causes. This clarity helps ensure that the trust operates in accordance with the creator's wishes.

2. **Guidance for Trustees:** The statement of purpose serves as a roadmap for trustees, guiding them in their duties and decision-making processes. By understanding the creator's intentions, trustees can effectively administer the trust and make decisions that align with the trust's objectives. This helps prevent misunderstandings or conflicts among trustees and

ensures consistent management of the trust over time.

3. **Beneficiary Understanding:** A trust statement of purpose can help beneficiaries understand the creator's intentions and expectations for the trust. By clearly articulating the purpose of the trust, beneficiaries can have a better understanding of their rights and entitlements, as well as the conditions or criteria for receiving distributions from the trust. This transparency fosters trust and cooperation among beneficiaries and trustees.

4. **Legal Clarity:** In legal proceedings or disputes involving the trust, a statement of purpose can provide valuable evidence of the creator's intentions. It can help clarify ambiguous provisions in the trust documents and support the interpretation of the trust by courts or legal authorities. This can be especially important in cases where the trust's terms are challenged or contested.

5. **Flexibility and Adaptability:** A trust statement of purpose can also provide flexibility for future changes or circumstances. It can include provisions allowing for amendments or modifications to the trust in response to changing needs, circumstances, or legal requirements. This ensures that the trust remains relevant and effective over time, even as circumstances evolve.

Overall, a trust statement of purpose is important because it provides clarity, guidance, and direction for the administration of the trust, helping to ensure that the creator's intentions are carried out effectively and that the trust serves its intended purpose for the benefit of beneficiaries. Check out the end of the book for an excerpt from my trust to get you thinking.

Step-by-Step Approach to Building, Growing and Protecting Wealth

Now, let's outline a step-by-step approach to building, growing and protecting wealth for future generations:

Step-by-Step Approach to Building Wealth with a Mindset of Abundance:

1. **Recognize the Battle:** Acknowledge the internal struggle between faith and fear in your journey. Understand that fear often stems from self-doubt and limiting beliefs, while faith is rooted in confidence and possibility.

2. **Choose Faith Over Fear:** Make a conscious decision to prioritize faith over fear. Recognize when fear creeps in and replace it with affirmations of confidence and belief in your abilities. Trust that you have the resilience and capability to overcome challenges and achieve your goals.

3. **Renew Your Mind:** Practice daily affirmations and positive self-talk to rewire your thoughts and beliefs. Focus on your strengths, past successes, and the abundance of opportunities available to you.

Surround yourself with positivity and inspiration to cultivate a mindset of abundance.

4. **Embrace Strategic Vision:** Develop a forward-thinking mindset by anticipating future trends and opportunities. Stay informed about market dynamics, emerging technologies, and consumer needs. Think strategically about how you can position yourself ahead of the curve to capitalize on emerging opportunities.

5. **Stay Agile and Adaptable:** Be prepared to pivot and adapt to changing circumstances. Entrepreneurship is dynamic, and success often requires flexibility and agility. Embrace change as an opportunity for growth and innovation.

6. **Invest in Continuous Learning:** Commit to lifelong learning and personal development. Invest in courses, workshops, and mentorship programs to expand your knowledge and skillset. Stay curious and open-minded, always seeking new ways to improve and innovate.

7. **Build a Support Network:** Surround yourself with mentors, advisors, and peers who believe in your vision and support your journey. Seek guidance and feedback from experienced entrepreneurs and financially literate professionals who can offer valuable insights and perspective.

8. **Take Bold Action:** Have the courage to take bold leaps and pursue your financial goals and entrepreneurial aspirations. Trust in your abilities and have confidence in your vision. Take calculated risks and

embrace failure as a learning opportunity on the path to success.

9. **Stay Persistent and Resilient:** Entrepreneurship is a journey filled with ups and downs. Stay persistent in pursuing your goals, even in the face of setbacks and challenges. Cultivate resilience and learn from failures, using them as steppingstones towards greater success.

10. **Celebrate Your Wins:** Acknowledge and celebrate your achievements along the way. Recognize the progress you've made and the milestones you've reached. Celebrating your wins boosts morale and motivation, fueling your continued pursuit of wealth and prosperity.

By following these steps and cultivating a mindset of abundance, you can overcome fear, seize opportunities, and build lasting wealth through financial literacy and entrepreneurship. Trust in yourself, stay focused on your goals, and embrace the journey with unwavering faith and determination.

Step-by-Step Approach to Building Wealth with Real Estate:

1. **Educate Yourself:** Start by immersing yourself in real estate literature, attending workshops, and seeking advice from experienced investors. Understanding the nuances of real estate investing, including market trends, financing options, and property management, is crucial for success.

2. **Set Clear Goals and Strategy:** Define your financial objectives, whether it's generating passive income, building equity through property appreciation, or both. Choose an investment strategy that aligns with your goals, whether it's buy-and-hold rentals, fix-and-flip renovations, or other approaches.

3. **Secure Financing:** Explore financing options such as traditional mortgages, private lenders, or partnerships to fund your real estate investments. Evaluate the risks and benefits of each option and choose the one that best suits your financial situation and investment strategy.

4. **Start Small and Scale Up:** Begin with smaller, manageable properties to gain experience and build confidence as an investor. As you become more comfortable with the process, gradually expand your portfolio by acquiring additional properties or pursuing larger investment opportunities.

5. **Build a Reliable Team:** Surround yourself with a team of trusted professionals, including real estate agents, contractors, property managers, and legal advisors. Having a reliable support network can help streamline the investment process and mitigate risks.

6. **Perform Due Diligence:** Conduct thorough research and analysis before making any investment decisions. Evaluate potential properties based on factors such as location, market demand, rental yields, renovation costs, and potential appreciation.

7. **Implement Efficient Property Management:** Develop effective property management systems to maximize rental income and minimize expenses. Stay proactive

in maintaining your properties, addressing tenant needs, and staying abreast of market developments.

8. **Monitor and Adjust:** Continuously monitor the performance of your real estate portfolio and be prepared to adapt your strategy as needed. Stay informed about market trends, economic indicators, and regulatory changes that may impact your investments.

9. **Reinvest Profits Wisely:** As your real estate portfolio grows, reinvest profits into additional properties or alternative investment vehicles to diversify your holdings and maximize returns. Consider leveraging equity from existing properties to finance new acquisitions or undertake value-adding renovations.

10. **Plan for the Long Term:** Building wealth through real estate is a marathon, not a sprint. Maintain a long-term perspective, stay disciplined in your investment approach, and be patient as you work towards achieving your financial goals.

By following these steps and remaining committed to your investment strategy, you can create a sustainable path to wealth accumulation and financial independence through real estate investing.

Step-by-Step Approach to Growing Wealth with Dividend Stocks:

1. **Educate Yourself:** Start by learning the fundamentals of dividend investing, including how dividends work, different types of dividend-paying stocks, and strategies for selecting quality dividend-paying companies. Take advantage of resources such as books, online courses, and financial websites to enhance your knowledge.

2. **Identify Blue-Chip Companies:** Research and identify established, industry-leading companies with a proven track record of reliable dividend payments. Look for companies with strong financials, consistent earnings growth, and a history of increasing dividends over time. Examples include Coca Cola (KO), Johnson & Johnson (JNJ), Target (TGT), and Walmart (WMT).

3. **Embrace Dividend Growth Investing:** Prioritize companies that not only pay dividends but also have a history of consistently increasing them annually. This strategy, known as dividend growth investing, ensures that your investment income keeps pace with inflation and grows over time. Examples of companies known for their dividend growth include IBM (IBM), Caterpillar (CAT), Exxon-Mobile (XOM), McDonald's (MCD), and Procter & Gamble (PG).

4. **Diversify Your Portfolio:** Spread your investments across multiple sectors and industries to mitigate risk and capture opportunities for growth. Consider allocating your portfolio across sectors such as

information technology, real estate, consumer staples, materials, financials, and healthcare. Diversification is key to building a resilient investment portfolio that can weather market fluctuations.

5. **Adopt a Long-Term Mindset:** Building generational wealth requires patience and discipline. Stay committed to your investment plan, even during periods of market volatility, and resist the temptation to engage in short-term speculation. Focus on accumulating quality dividend-paying stocks and holding them for the long term to benefit from compounding returns.

6. **Harness Cumulative Dividends:** Reinvest dividends to harness the power of compounding and accelerate wealth accumulation over time. By reinvesting dividends, you can purchase additional shares of dividend-paying stocks, which, in turn, generate more dividends. This snowball effect can significantly increase your investment returns and create a steady stream of income for the future.

7. **Understand Tax Implications:** Be mindful of the tax implications of dividend investing and develop strategies to minimize tax liabilities. Depending on your tax bracket and investment accounts (such as taxable brokerage accounts, retirement accounts, or tax-deferred accounts), dividends may be subject to different tax rates. Consult with a tax advisor or financial planner to optimize your investment strategy for tax efficiency.

By following these steps and staying disciplined in your approach to dividend investing, you can build wealth steadily over time and create a lasting legacy of prosperity for future generations.

Step-by-Step Approach to Protecting Wealth:

1. **Transfer Investment Funds:** Begin by transferring investment funds from retirement accounts like IRAs and 401(k)s to a suitable fixed indexed annuity. Choose an annuity with favorable terms, such as an 18% bonus and options for tax-deferred growth and flexible withdrawal options. This allocates the risk of any market downturn from you to the insurance company, but you still get to capitalize on gains from the stock market.

2. **Utilize Fixed Indexed Annuity Interest for Insurance:** Once your funds are invested in the fixed indexed annuity, leverage the interest earned annually to fund insurance policies that align with your financial goals. Establish a high yield savings account to receive annuity withdrawals automatically and allocate funds to various insurance policies, including whole life, over-funded, and indexed universal life policies.

3. **Establish a Will and Trust:** Finally, establish a comprehensive estate plan, including a will and trust, to protect and preserve your wealth for future generations. Make sure to fund the trust by transferring ownership of specific assets to the trustee of the trust. Carefully craft a trust statement of purpose to articulate your intentions, values, and objectives, guiding

trustees and beneficiaries in the administration of your estate.

Conclusion

Building and safeguarding generational wealth is a journey that requires careful planning, informed decision making, and strategic execution. By gathering your financial information, defining your goals, and creating a comprehensive financial plan, you lay the groundwork for a secure and prosperous future. Consult with trusted professionals, explore investment options, and leverage tools like annuities and insurance policies to protect and grow your wealth. With dedication, diligence, and foresight, you can create a lasting financial legacy that benefits your family for generations to come.

CHAPTER 13:
Securing Your Legacy: A Call To Action

"If you want to change your life you have to change your strategy, you have to change your story, and you have to change."

—**Anthony Robbins**, *MONEY Master the Game: 7 Simple Steps to Financial Freedom*

As we reach the conclusion of this journey toward building and protecting generational wealth, it's crucial to reflect on the knowledge gained and the actions needed to secure a prosperous future for ourselves and our loved ones. Throughout this book, we've explored the powerful tools and strategies available for those seeking to break the cycle of financial inequality and create lasting legacies of wealth and success.

Education has been highlighted as the cornerstone of our journey, empowering us with the knowledge and skills needed to navigate the complexities of the financial world. By investing in our education and continuously seeking to expand our financial literacy, we position ourselves for success and open doors to opportunities that can propel us toward our goals.

Real estate has been shown to be a powerful wealth building tool, offering opportunities for passive income, capital appreciation, and asset diversification. By strategically investing in real estate and leveraging the benefits of homeownership, we can create tangible assets that serve as pillars of our financial stability.

Financial investment accounts, including retirement plans and brokerage accounts, offer pathways to wealth accumulation and long-term financial growth. By diligently contributing to these accounts and making informed investment decisions, we can harness the power of compounding returns and build wealth over time.

Insurance has emerged as a critical safeguard against unexpected setbacks, providing protection for our families and assets in times of need. By securing adequate insurance coverage, we can mitigate risks and ensure that our loved ones are taken care of, regardless of what the future may hold.

In addition to these corporate and financial vehicles, we've explored the importance of estate planning, including wills, trusts, and other legal mechanisms for transferring wealth to future generations. By proactively planning for the future and establishing clear directives for the distribution of our assets, we can ensure that our legacies endure for generations to come.

As we conclude this book, I urge you to take action and implement the strategies outlined within these pages. Commit to lifelong learning and prioritize your education, seek out opportunities to protect your assets through insurance, and diligently invest in your financial future through strategic use of investment accounts and real estate.

Above all, remember that building generational wealth is

not just about accumulating riches for ourselves, but about creating opportunities for future generations to thrive and prosper. By taking control of our financial destinies today, we can pave the way for a brighter tomorrow for ourselves, our families, and our communities.

I challenge you to embrace the journey toward financial empowerment and to seize the opportunities that lie ahead. Together, let us build and protect generational wealth that will stand as a testament to our resilience, ingenuity, and unwavering commitment to a better future.

Thank you for joining me on this journey and may your path toward financial success be paved with prosperity, abundance, and lasting legacy.

With warmest regards,

Charlie Bingham Jr.

Financial Information

The more you can share during your conversation with a financial advisor, the better. You can use the following checklists and sample forms to prepare for your conversation. Be prepared to discuss:

- Fixed assets like a home or vehicle
- Liabilities like a mortgage, credit card, or loan
- Investments, life insurance, retirement, or savings
- Wills, trusts, or other generational transfer vehicles

INFORMATION FOR WILLS AND TRUST

Part I:
Personal Information

Client's Legal Name _______________________________________
(name most often used to title property and accounts)

Also Known As _______________________________________
(other names used to title property and accounts)

Birth date ___ SS# ___ US Citizen? ___ Home Address ___ City ___ State ___ Zip ___

Home Telephone _______ County of Residence ___ Business Telephone _______

Employer _______________________ Position _______________________

Business Address _______________ City _______ State ___ Zip _______

E-mail Address _______ ☐ It is okay to communicate with me via my E-mail address.

Date of Marriage _______________________
Client's Spouse or Second
Grantor's Legal Name _______________________________________
(name most often used to title property and accounts)

Also Known As _______________________________________
(other names used to title property and accounts)

Birth date ___ SS# ___ US Citizen? ___ Home Address ___ City ___ State ___ Zip ___

Home Telephone _______ County of Residence ___ Business Telephone _______

Employer _______________________ Position _______________________

Business Address _______________ City _______ State ___ Zip _______

E-mail Address _______________________

Children and Other Family Members

Name	Birth date	Parent or Relationship

____ __________ __________

Comments: ____

____ __________ __________

Comments: ____

____ __________ __________

Comments: ____

____ __________ __________

Comments: ____

____ __________ __________

Comments: ____

Advisors

Name	Telephone

Personal Attorney ___________________________________ __________

Accountant ___________________________________ __________

Financial Advisor ___________________________________ __________

Life Insurance Agent ___________________________________ __________

Your Concerns

Please rate the following as to how important they are to you:
(H high concern, S some concerned, L low concern, N/A no concern or not applicable)

Description

Level of Concern

Client   Spouse

Desire to get affairs in order and create a comprehensive plan to manage affairs in case of death or disability.

Providing for and protecting a spouse.

Providing for and protecting children.

Providing for and protecting grandchildren.

Disinheriting a family member.

Providing for charities at the time of death.

Plan for the transfer and survival of a family business.

Avoiding or reducing your estate taxes.

Avoiding probate.

Reduce administration costs at time of your death.

Avoiding a conservatorship ("living probate") in case of a disability. Avoiding will contests or other disputes upon death.

Protecting assets from lawsuits or creditors.

Preserving the privacy of affairs in case of disability or at time of death from business competitors, predators, dishonest persons and curiosity seekers.

Plan for a child with disabilities or special needs, such as medical or learning disabilities.

Protecting children's inheritance from the possibility of failed marriages.

Protect children's inheritance in the event of a surviving spouse's remarriage. Provide that your death shall not be unnecessarily prolonged by artificial means or measures.

Other Concerns (Please list below):

Important Family Questions

(Please check "Yes" or "No" for your answer)	Yes	No
Are you (or your spouse) receiving Social Security, disability, or other governmental benefits? *Describe.*		
Are you (or your spouse) making payments pursuant to a divorce or property settlement order? *Please furnish a copy.*		
If married, have you and your spouse signed a pre- or post-marriage contract? *Please furnish a copy.*		
Have you (or your spouse) been widowed? *If a federal estate tax return or a state death tax return was filed, please furnish a copy.*		
Have you (or your spouse) ever filed federal or state gift tax returns? *Please furnish copies of these returns.*		
Have you (or your spouse) completed previous will, trust, or estate planning? *Please furnish copies of these documents.*		
Do you support any charitable organizations now that you wish to make provisions for at the time of your death? *If so, please explain below.*		
Are there any other charitable organizations you wish to make provisions for at the time of your death? *If so, please explain below.*		
If married, have you lived in any of the following states while married to each other? *Arizona, California, Idaho, Louisiana, Nevada, New Mexico, Texas, Washington, or Wisconsin*		
Are you (or your spouse) currently the beneficiary of anyone else's trust? *If so, please explain below.*		
Do any of your children have special educational, medical, or physical needs?		
Do any of your children receive governmental support or benefits?		
Do you provide primary or other major financial support to adult children or others?		

ADDITIONAL INFORMATION

Part II:
Property Information

Instructions for completing the Property Information checklist:

General Headings

This **Property Information** checklist helps you list all the property you own and what it is worth. If you do not own property under a particular heading, just leave that section blank. Under certain headings, you may own more property than can be listed on this checklist. If so, attach extra sheets of paper to list your additional property.

Type

Immediately after the heading for each kind of property is a brief explanation of what property you should list under that heading.

"Owner" of Property

How you own your property is **extremely important** for purposes of properly designing and implementing your estate plan. For each property, please indicate how the property is titled.

Real Property

Any interest in real estate including your family residence, vacation home, timeshare, vacant land, etc.

General Description and/or Address	Owner	Market Value	Loan Balance
_________________________	_______	_______	_______
_________________________	_______	_______	_______
_________________________	_______	_______	_______
	Total		_______

Furniture and Personal Effects

List separately only major personal effects such as jewelry, collections, antiques, furs, and all other valuable non-business personal property *(indicate type below and **give a lump sum value for miscellaneous**, less valuable items.).*

Type or Description	Owner	Market Value
Miscellaneous Furniture and Household Effects (Total)	_______	_______
_________________________	_______	_______
_________________________	_______	_______
_________________________	_______	_______
_________________________	*Total*	_______

Automobiles, Boats, and RVs

For each motor vehicle, boat, RV, etc. please list the following: description, how titled, market value and encumbrance:

____

____

____

____

Bank Accounts

TYPE: Checking Account "CA", Savings Account "SA", Certificates of Deposit "CD", Money Market "MM" (*indicate type below*).
<u>*Do not include IRAs or 401(k)s here*</u>
Note: If Account is in your name (or your spouse's name) for the benefit of a minor, please specify and give minor's name.

Name of Institution and account number	Type	Owner	Amount
		Total	

Stocks and Bonds

List any and all stocks and bonds you own. <u>If held in a brokerage account, lump them together under each account.</u>
(indicate type below)

Stocks, Bonds or Investment Accounts	Type	Acct. Number	Owner	Amount
_____	___	___	___	___
_____	___	___	___	___
_____	___	___	___	___
_____	___	___	___	___
_____	___	___	___	___
_____	___	___	___	___
_____	___	___	___	___

Total _____

Life Insurance Policies and Annuities

TYPE: Term, whole life, split dollar, group life, annuity.

ADDITIONAL INFORMATION: Insurance company, type, face amount (death benefit), whose life is insured, who owns the policy, the current beneficiaries, who pays the premium, and who is the life insurance agent.

____

____

____

____

____

____

____

Total _______________________

Retirement Plans

TYPE: Pension (P), Profit Sharing (PS), H.R. 10, IRA, SEP, 401(K).

ADDITIONAL INFORMATION: Describe the type of plan, the plan name, the current value of the plan, and any other pertinent information.

____

____

____

____

____

Total _______________________

Business Interests

TYPE: General and Limited Partnerships, Sole Proprietorships, privately-owned corporations, professional corporations, oil interests, farm, and ranch interests.

ADDITIONAL INFORMATION: Give a description of the interests, who has the interest, your ownership in the interests, and the estimated value of the interests.

____

____

____

____

____

Total _______________________

Money Owed to You

TYPE: Mortgages or promissory notes payable **to you**, or other moneys owed to you.

Name of Debtor	Date of Note	Maturity Date	Owed to	Current Balance
_______________	_______	_______	_______	_______
_______________	_______	_______	_______	_______
_______________	_______	_______	_______	_______
_______________	_______	_______	_______	_______
			Total	_______

Anticipated Inheritance, Gift, or Lawsuit Judgment

Gifts or inheritances that you expect to receive at some time in the future; or moneys that you anticipate receiving through a judgment in a lawsuit. **Describe in appropriate detail.**

Description ____

____

*Total estimated value*_______________

Other Assets

Other property is any property that you have that does not fit into any listed category.

Type	Owner	Value
_______________________	______	______
_______________________	______	______
_______________________	______	______
_______________________	______	______
_______________________	*Total*	______

Summary of Values

Assets	Client	Spouse	Total Value
Real Property			
Furniture and Personal Effects			
Automobiles, RVs, and Boats			
Bank Accounts			
Stocks and Bonds			
Life Insurance and Annuities			
Retirement Plans			
Business Interests			
Money Owed to You			
Anticipated Inheritance, etc.			
Other Assets			
Total Assets			

** Joint Property values enter 1/2 in client's column and 1/2 in spouse's column.*

Part III

Design Information

PERSONS TO ACT FOR YOU:

GUARDIAN FOR MINOR CHILDREN: If you have any children under the age of 18, list in order of preference who you wish to be **guardian**.

Name and Address
Relationship

____

____

____

INITIAL TRUSTEE(S): Usually, the Maker will be the Trustee of his or her own trust. Often, both spouses, jointly. Allows you to continue to jointly control your assets as before.

Name and Address
Relationship

____

____

____

DISABILITY TRUSTEE: If you were unable to make
decisions for yourself, who
would you want to make
decisions for you with regard
to your property and assets?

FOR CLIENT
> **Name and Address**
> **Relationship**

____
____
____

FOR SPOUSE
> **Name and Address**
> **Relationship**

____
____
____

DEATH TRUSTEE: After your death, who do
you want carrying out your
instructions, for distribution
to and, if desired, management
of property for your
beneficiaries?

FOR CLIENT
   Name and Address
   Relationship

____

____

____

FOR SPOUSE
   Name and Address
   Relationship

____

____

____

POWER OF ATTORNEY: If you were unable to make financial decisions for yourself, who would you want to make those decisions for you?

CLIENT'S AGENT

    Name and Address
        Relationship   **Instructions or Guidelines**

_______________________   _______________________

_______________________   _______________________

_______________________   _______________________

SPOUSE'S AGENT

    Name and Address
        Relationship   **Instructions or Guidelines**

_______________________   _______________________

_______________________   _______________________

_______________________   _______________________

Do you want to authorize your Financial Agent to make gifts on your behalf during any period of time you are incapacitated?

         Client: ☐ Yes ☐ No   Spouse: ☐ Yes ☐ No

Gifting Power Details: _______________________

____

LIVING WILL: Do you want to provide that the moment of your death not be unnecessarily prolonged by artificial means or measures? Do you want to provide that your organs and tissues should be made available for transplant purposes?

HEALTH CARE: If you were unable to make decisions for yourself, who would you want to make decisions for you with regard to your medical treatment?

CLIENT'S AGENT

Name and Address
Relationship   Instructions or Guidelines

_______________________   _______________________

_______________________   _______________________

_______________________   _______________________

SPOUSE'S AGENT

Name and Address
Relationship   Instructions or Guidelines

_______________________   _______________________

_______________________   _______________________

_______________________   _______________________

Do you want to authorize your Medical Agent to take whatever steps are necessary to keep you in a personal residence rather than nursing home?

Client: ☐ Yes ☐ No   Spouse: ☐ Yes ☐ No

Do you want to provide that upon certification by 2 physicians of need for psychological or substance treatment, Agent may arrange for voluntary admission?

Client: ☐ Yes ☐ No   Spouse: ☐ Yes ☐ No

In making distributions during any period of time the client is incapacitated, the successor Trustee shall give primary consideration to:

☐ Disabled spouse, the needs of others.

☐ Disabled spouse and other spouse, and then needs of others.

☐ Disabled spouse needs and the needs of others equally.

DISTRIBUTIONS OF PERSONAL PROPERTY AND SPECIFIC GIFTS

USE OF PERSONAL PROPERTY MEMORANDUM: Do you want to provide that your personal property will be distributed pursuant to a written list you may prepare later?

☐ Yes ☐ No

Any property not listed on the memorandum should be distributed to:

FOR CLIENT:

☐ Spouse, then children equally.
☐ Children

☐ Spouse, then to balance of trust.
☐ Spouse, then other named individuals.

☐ To the balance of the trust.
☐ Other named individuals. List on next line.

FOR SPOUSE: ______________________________

☐ Spouse, then children equally.
☐ Spouse, then to balance of trust.
☐ Spouse, then other named individuals.

☐ Children
☐ To the balance of the trust.
☐ Other named individuals. List on next line.

SPECIFIC GIFTS: List any specific gifts of real estate or cash gifts you wish to make to either individuals or charities. Indicate whether these gifts are to be made even if the other spouse is alive.

FOR CLIENT:

Individual or Charity	Amount or Property	Contingent on Spouse predeceasing?

____

____

____

____

____

____

____

____

____

FOR SPOUSE:

Individual or Charity	Amount or Property	Contingent on Spouse predeceasing?

____

____

____

____

____

____

____

____

____

PROVIDING FOR THE SURVIVING SPOUSE UPON DEATH OF FIRST SPOUSE TO DIE

- ☐ **TO SURVIVING SPOUSE WITHOUT TAX PLANNING:** We recognize this does not provide any tax planning which may result in our beneficiaries paying significant optional estate taxes.
- ☐ All to surviving spouse.
- ☐ _______% to surviving spouse.
- ☐ Minimum allowed by law to surviving spouse.
- ☐ **DIVIDE INTO MARITAL AND FAMILY TRUSTS:** Designed to maximize estate tax savings. To accomplish this, an amount up to the applicable exclusion amount (currently $5,000,000) will be transferred to the Family Trust and the balance, if any, to the Marital Trust. This is sometimes referred to as "A/B Trust Planning". The Marital Trust is sometimes referred to as the "A Trust" or "QTIP Trust". The Family Trust is sometimes referred to as the "B Trust", "By-Pass Trust" or "Credit Shelter Trust". Also provides protection for surviving spouse from creditors and predators. You decide how much control you want the surviving spouse to have. In the event of remarriage protects property for your heirs from a new spouse in case of death or divorce.

DESIGN OF MARITAL SHARE:

☐ **OUTRIGHT:** We want to leave property outright to the surviving spouse. We recognize that this offers no protection from creditors or predators. Allows surviving spouse to leave property to whomever surviving spouse wants. Also allows a new spouse to possibly make claim on property in case of death or divorce.

☐ **GENERAL APPOINTMENT TRUST:** All income and principal are available to the surviving spouse upon demand. The surviving spouse is free to do as he or she pleases. This would include the ability to remove all property in the Marital Share from the trust.

☐ **ALL INCOME – PRINCIPAL FOR NEEDS:** All income is distributed to surviving spouse; principal is available for his or her needs (health, education, and maintenance).

☐ **ONLY INCOME:** Only income is distributed to surviving spouse. Principal is not available to the surviving spouse.

DESIGN OF FAMILY SHARE:

☐ **ALL INCOME – PRINCIPAL FOR NEEDS:** All income is distributed to surviving spouse; principal is available for needs (health, education, and maintenance).

Are descendants permissible beneficiaries of principal?

☐ **INCOME AND PRINCIPAL FOR NEEDS:** All income and principal is available for needs. Income may be accumulated and not distributed.

Are descendants permissible beneficiaries of income and/or principal?

☐ **ONLY INCOME:** Only income is distributed to surviving spouse. Principal is not available to the surviving spouse.

WHO IS RESPONSIBLE FOR DETERMINING LIFETIME DISTRIBUTIONS: Is surviving spouse the sole trustee with a right to appoint cotrustees (surviving spouse then determines the management and distributions for his or her needs)?

Do you wish to name someone to be the cotrustee with the surviving spouse?

☐ **LIMITED POWER OF APPOINTMENT:** Do you want the surviving spouse to be able to modify the way property is distributed upon the surviving spouse's death?

If so, to whom may the surviving spouse distribute your property:

☐ Your descendants
☐ Your descendants and their spouses
☐ Your descendants and charities
☐ Your descendants, their spouses and charities
☐ Anyone, no limitations

DIVISION OF PROPERTY UPON DEATH OF SECOND SPOUSE TO DIE

- ☐ **DIVIDE EQUALLY BETWEEN OUR CHILDREN AND THE DESCENDANTS OF ANY DECEASED CHILDREN:**
- ☐ **DIVIDE AMONG NAMED INDIVIDUALS and/ or CHARITIES:**

HOW AND WHEN TO DISTRIBUTE MY PROPERTY:

- ☐ **DISTRIBUTE OUTRIGHT TO OUR BENEFICIARIES:** Provides no protection from creditors, predators, or from themselves.
- ☐ **STRUCTURED TRUST:** You determine how long the property is to remain in trust. During the period of time the property is held in trust it is available to the beneficiary for needs (health, education and maintenance). You may give written instructions to the trustee outlining guidelines to follow in determining the beneficiary's needs. You may provide for a staggered distribution of principal. For example:. 1/3 at age 30 and balance at age 40. You decide who will manage the property and to carry out your distribution instructions. Does the beneficiary have a right to be a cotrustee and/or choose his or her own cotrustee? You decide how the trust is designed. List your desires:

REMOTE CONTINGENT BENEFICIARY: Who do you want to receive your property in the remote event that no one listed above is alive to receive your property? Determining the remote contingent beneficiary is not so important that it should cause you to delay completion of your entire estate plan. It can always be changed at a later date.

In the remote event no one listed above is alive to receive my property I want my property distributed as follows:

- ☐ To each spouse's heirs-at-law.
- ☐ One-half to Client's heirs-at-law and one-half to Spouse's heirs at law.
- ☐ To the following named individuals and/or charities:

OTHER ITEMS TO INCLUDE OR DISCUSS: Obviously your estate plan should address all your hopes, fears, and wishes. Please list any other items you want included or want to discuss:

____

____

____

____

____

____

____

____

Trust Statement of Purpose

The Premise is the truth about the world as I know it. It's the way things are.

The Vision is the way I see myself and my family having an impact on the world and the way things are.

The Purpose is the reason why the Vision is important.

The Strategy is how to implement the Vision.

Family Premise:

- United we stand and divided we fall.
- People will forget what you say or do but people will never forget how you made them feel.
- Always remember who you are and whose you are.

Family Vision:

- I envision a united family where there is clear, transparent and constant conversation among family members.
- I envision a family that is transparent with the next generation about generational curses and mistakes made by the previous generation.
- I envision a family that has open, honest communication and does not shy away from difficult conversations and there is freedom to express emotions openly.

Family Purpose:

- Through this trust you have been blessed with the financial means and opportunity to pursue your purpose and dreams of adding value to the world by making it better.
- Family is supposed to make each other better because iron sharpens iron.
- Family is meant to be fruitful and multiply soldiers for Christ.

Family Strategy:

- Family should focus on educating the next generation even if that means homeschooling to ensure they are not trained to be employees or workers but rather producers of value for their family and community and purposeful fulfillers of purpose.
- Anyone marrying into the family should have a strategy to assist their family in making it to heaven. If they don't have their own personal relationship with God that is seen through their actions, then run!
- Family should commit to mental wellness by finding a good therapist when needed to deal with stress, sadness, trauma, or other negative emotions that will inevitably happen in life.

Family To Do List:

- Create a list of your family's core values.
- Use the values to create a family mission statement.
- Make sure you have a family meeting where you discuss (everyone gets a say) and write down your answers to the following questions:

  o What does it mean to be a member of this family?

  o What makes this family unique or special compared to other families?

  o What is the purpose of our family?

- o   How do we want to treat each other?
- o   What traditions do we want to keep and create?
- o   What things are truly important to us as a family?
- o   What are the principles we want this family to follow?
- o   What other families do we admire? Why?

Spiritual Premise:

- Everything in existence is a manifestation of the one living being we call God. Everything is God.
- God loves you. You are fearfully and wonderfully made. God can use you for His purpose no matter how flawed you are.
- You are entitled to know that two entities occupy your body. One of these entities is motivated by and responds to the impulse of fear. The other is motivated by and responds to the impulse of faith. Will you be guided by faith or will you allow fear to overtake you?

Spiritual Vision:

- I envision a world where people understand that you brought nothing in this world, and you can't take anything out so don't place too much of a value on material possessions.

- I envision a world where people understand what the will of the Lord is for their life.
- I envision a world where people understand that all people were made in the image and likeness of God.

Spiritual Purpose:

- The whole duty of man is to fear God and keep his commandments.
- We know that a man is not justified by the works of the law, but by the faith of Jesus Christ.
- We know that God's compassion for us never fails, and his compassions are new every morning.

Spiritual Strategy:

- The mind acts upon one's dominating, or most pronounced desires. There is no escape from this fact. It is a fact indeed. "Be careful what you set your heart upon, for it surely shall be yours.
- Pray not for more of this world's goods and greater blessings, but to be worthy of that which you already have.
- Be definite in everything you do and never leave unfinished thoughts in the mind. Form the habit of reaching definite decisions on all subjects.

Spiritual To Do List:

- Spiritual practical rules to abide by:
  - Do your own thinking on all occasions.
  - Analyze temporary defeat, no matter of what nature or cause, and extract from it the seed of an equivalent advantage.
  - Recognize that your greatest asset is time, the only thing except the power of thought which you own outright, and the one thing which can be shaped into whatever material things you want. Budget your time so none of it is wasted.
- Think on these things:
  - whatever is true,
  - whatever is honorable,
  - whatever is just,
  - whatever is pure,
  - whatever is lovely,
  - whatever is commendable, if there is any excellence, if there is anything worthy of praise, think about these things.

Philosophical Premise:

- Everyone dies but not everyone truly lives.
- You are the master of your destiny. You can influence,

direct and control your own environment. You can make your life what you want it to be.

- Your only limitation is the one which you set up in your own mind.

Philosophical Vision:

- I envision a world where people understand the law of attraction and are mindful of their thoughts, character and deeds.

Philosophical Purpose:

- The most practical of all methods for controlling the mind is the habit of keeping it busy with a definite purpose, backed by a definite plan. A man whose mind is filled with fear not only destroys his own chances of intelligent action, but he transmits these destructive vibrations to the minds of all who come in contact with him, and destroys, also, their chances.
- We must never stop dreaming. Dreams provide nourishment for the soul, just as a meal does for the body. Many times in our lives we see our dreams shattered and our desires frustrated, but we have to continue dreaming. If we don't, our soul dies, and agape cannot reach it.
- Before we can stand out, we must first get clear on what we stand for.

Philosophical Strategy:

- Learn to question yourself: Why this anger or resentment? Where does this incessant need for attention come from? Under such scrutiny, your emotions will lose their hold on you. You will begin to think for yourself instead of reacting to what others give you.

- The first step toward becoming rational is to understand our fundamental irrationality. There are two factors that should render this more palatable to our egos: nobody is exempt from the irresistible effect of emotions on the mind, not even the wisest among us; and to some extent irrationality is a function of the structure of our brains and is wired into our very nature by the way we process emotions. Being irrational is almost beyond our control.

- You must realize the dominating thoughts of your mind will eventually reproduce themselves in outward, physical action, and gradually transform themselves into physical reality, therefore, you will concentrate your thoughts for thirty minutes daily, upon the task of thinking of the person you intend to become, thereby creating in your mind a clear mental picture of that person.

Philosophical To Do List:

- Speak with integrity. Say only what you mean. Avoid using the word to speak against yourself or to gossip about others. Use your power of your word in the direction of truth and love.
- Make sure to always take time to yourself. Two solo trips abroad will help you know more about yourself and get comfortable being uncomfortable.
- Life will eventually life and you have to be able to deal with the ups and downs remembering who you are and whose you are will help you handle these moments.

Educational Premise:

- Knowledge is only potential power. It becomes power only when, and if, it is organized into definite plans of action, and directed to a definite end.
- The greatest obstacle to knowledge is not ignorance; it is the illusion of knowledge.
- Once you have learned how to ask questions—relevant and appropriate and substantial questions—you have learned how to learn and no one can keep you from learning whatever you want or need to know.

Educational Vision:

- I envision a world where people understand that a supportive environment is essential to develop spiritual maturity and academic excellence.
- I envision a world where people understand the importance of educating themselves and sharing what they learn with others to inspire.

Educational Purpose:

- The goal is not simply for you to cross the finish line, but to see how many people you can inspire to run with you.
- People have a right to their own opinions, but not to their own facts. Evidence must be located, not created, and opinions not backed by evidence cannot be given much weight.

Educational Strategy:

- Think for yourself and when you hold an opinion that is popular, seek out contrary opinions to learn.
- Aim to be a learn it all and not a know it all.
- Surround yourself with people that are smarter than you.

Educational To Do List:

- Read at least 20 books in the Trust Book List.
- You can learn something from anyone so be careful not to be too haughty to where you miss a chance to learn.

Finance Premise:

- If my sense of security lies in my reputation or in the things I have, my life will be in a constant state of threat and jeopardy that these possessions may be lost or stolen or devalued.
- It costs nothing to ask wise advice from a good friend.
- Dependency is a habit that is so easy to acquire. Once you give in, it is like a prison you enter that you cannot ever leave. If we succumb to the illusion and the comfort of a paycheck, we then neglect to build self-reliant skills and merely postpone the day of reckoning when we are forced to fend for ourselves.

Financial Vision:

- I envision a world where money is no longer the primary reason or excuse for people doing or not doing anything.
- I envision a world where my family grows wealthy

from understanding the financial premises above and grow wealthy from accomplishing their Soul Purpose and serving others.

- I envision a world where money is put in the proper place, behind purpose.

Financial Purpose:

- Your financial requirements or wants have nothing whatever to do with your WORTH. Your value is established entirely by your ability to render useful service or your capacity to induce others to render such service.

- I can focus on what is important and I work because I want to, never because I have to in order to make money. This creates clarity and allows for the mission to be the driver. My family feels secure and their thoughts can focus on happiness and creativity when money flows. I can expand my reach, my business, my education, and initially it grab's people's attention so they can hear the real message. It allows me to be a leader in a time of crisis, not a follower. When money is not the primary concern , the other areas of wealth are not more possible to focus on, to build. This creates conditions of peace and growth, and solves the problems that many face.

- Our wise acts accompany us through life to please us and to help us. Just as surely, our unwise acts follow us to plague and torment us. Alas, they cannot be forgotten. In the front rank of the torments that do follow us are the memories of the things we should have done, of the opportunities which came to us and we took not.

Financial Strategy:

- A part of all I earn is mine to keep. Say it in the morning when you first arise. Say it at noon. Say it at night. Say it each hour of every day. Say it to yourself until the words stand out like letters of fire across the sky.
- Work with the proper people. People that want to live their Soul Purpose to impact humanity.
- A primary investment strategy is to impact the right people and create ways to impact them as much as possible. Always have contracts and agreements before moving forward on any investment. Before investing, always consider the amount of time it will take. Invest in people. Invest in venues and into the things that will bring forth your vision. For me, it was to uplift and enlighten humanity spiritually and financially. Make sure you have clean accounting books, review weekly reports and income statements, and keep separate accounts to store money for yourself, when you do things others would normally get paid for. Have great resources when it comes to people that are willing to educate you and expand your investing universe.

Financial To Do List:

1. Get crystal clear on your financial status. NOW! And always!
2. Save a minimum of 18% of every check from now on.
3. Don't spend money to impress other people that are probably not thinking about you!

Trustee Letter of Wishes

Purposes: It is my express intention that my trust provide the maximum legal protection of the assets held in trust against the claims of any person. The other purposes are:

1. To eliminate or reduce estate taxes and ensure the transfer of generational wealth with as little taxation as possible.

2. To educate trust beneficiaries in financial management and ensure that beneficiaries get a head start in life.

3. To ensure the transfer of knowledge to the beneficiaries and future generations.

4. To ensure the transfer of financial security and stability to future generations.

Overview on Distributions: This letter is to express our wishes to you when exercising discretion as to making or not making distributions to beneficiaries. We appreciate that our wishes do not bind you in any way and that you remain free to make distributions as you see fit in the exercise of your discretion. We have no understanding or agreement with any of you with respect to distributions, and this letter is not meant to establish any such understanding or agreement. The contents of this letter are not intended to constitute terms of any trust and are not intended to establish or imply any standard to guide any fiduciary in exercising discretion. These wishes are for your consideration to the extent that you deem advisable under the circumstances. In general, it is our wish that our assets remain protected over time from the reach of any creditor or potential creditor of any descendant of ours, including, but not limited to, a spouse or former spouse. **Please precondition any distribution on the beneficiary's undertaking to enter into a valid marital property agreement or valid choice of governing marital property law that, in your judgement, would serve to protect the distribution(s) from the claims of a spouse or a former spouse.** In administering these trusts, you would do well as trustees if you would coordinate among yourselves when a distribution request is made by a beneficiary or when one of you perceives a need to act. Furthermore, when you determine to make distributions, we would request that you keep in mind the tax-sensitivity of these trusts. The trust is not exempt from generation-skipping transfer tax. Therefore, it would be tax-advantageous if distributions were made first from non-exempt trusts.

Specific Guidance on Distribution of Trust Funds: In exercising the discretion granted to the trustee(s), the trustees must consider the following values, which I wish each of my descendants to emulate:

- Spiritual enlightment and fulfillment of life's purpose to do good works and add value to human kind.
- The pursuit of higher education culminating in a four-year degree from an accredited U.S. college or university or the foreign equivalent.
- Healthy lifestyle choices, including avoiding abuse of or dependence on alcohol, legal or illegal drugs (other than as prescribed by the beneficiary's physician).

- Fiscal responsibility and the avoidance of excessive debt.
- Gainful employment, including employment in the arts, academia, or the helping professions and military service.
- Care for minor, disabled, and elderly family members.
- Support of charitable organizations.

Accordingly, my wishes as it pertains to distributions are as follows:

1. Prior to the Initial Beneficiaries turning 18 years of age, the legal guardian shall be provided with an annual income of $50,000 solely for the benefit of the Initial Beneficiaries. If an adult beneficiary has sufficient maturity and has demonstrated prudence with financial affairs after turning 18, the Trustees may distribute a one-time lump sum of $25,000 to each of the Initial Beneficiaries to use as they see fit.

2. Beneficiaries may request a one-time $5,000 distribution to purchase the books on the Trust Book List. Beneficiaries may also be eligible to request an additional $25,000 distribution if they read the books in the Trust Book List and provide to the Trustees for their consideration written evidence (*i.e.,* notebooks or digital files) of chapter summaries of each book and new word definitions for a minimum of 20 books. This written evidence shall become the property of the trust for historical purposes.

3. Beneficiaries upon reaching the age of 10 shall have over-funded whole life insurance policies with an annual premium of $10,000 taken out for them by

the Trust. The policy should be fully funded after 10 years so that no more premiums shall be due. The Trust should pay the premiums directly to the insurance company and the trust should be made as the primary beneficiary with the beneficiary considered a secondary beneficiary.

4. Beneficiaries shall be eligible for a one-time $15,000 Educational Loan paid directly to an accredited institution with the expectation that the beneficiary will pay back the loan within 10 years to the Trust with a deferred 2% interest that accrues on the 5th year of such loan.

5. Beneficiaries shall be eligible for a one-time $15,000 First Time Home Buyer Loan for an initial down payment with the expectation that the beneficiary will pay back the loan within 20 years to the Trust with a deferred 2% interest that accrues on the 3rd year of such loan.

6. Beneficiaries shall be eligible for a one-time $20,000 Business Loan for where the beneficiary presents the Trustees with a valid business plan (that Trustees in their sole discretion agree is worthy of the loan) with the expectation that the beneficiary will pay back the loan with 5% interest over 10 years.

7. Beneficiaries shall be eligible for a one-time $10,000 distribution to be paid directly to a health care facility for medical or psychological treatment when it may be warranted by an addiction or other harmful condition.

8. Beneficiaries shall be eligible for a one-time $2,500 distribution to be paid directly to a law firm to pay

the legal and other professional costs associated with the beneficiary's planning of his or her own estate plan, with a view to appropriate structures for the succession of wealth and wise tax planning for multiple generations.

In summary, please see the attached Statement of Purpose for more details on the principles and values I would like to use this Trust to pass on to future generations.

Sincerely yours,

Charlie Bingham Jr.

TRUST BOOK READING LIST

Spiritual Books:

1. The Holy Bible
2. The Apocrypha: The Complete Volume Including the Books of Enoch, Jubilees, and Jasher by Joseph Lumpkin
3. The Books of Enoch by Joseph Lumpkin
4. Outwitting the Devil by Napoleon Hill
5. The Case for Christ by Lee Strobel
6. How Africa Shaped the Christian Mind: Rediscovering the African Seedbed of Western Christianity by Thomas C. Oden
7. Hebrews to Negroes Volume I-III by Ronald Dalton Jr.
8. Kebra Nagast (The Glory of Kings) by Miguel F. Brooks
9. The Africans Who Wrote the Bible by Nana Banchie Darkwah
10. The Bible is Black History by Dr. Theron D. Williams
11. How We Got the Bible by Neil R. Lightfoot
12. Feeding the Soul by Tabitha Brown
13. Early Christian Doctrines by J.N.D. Kelly
14. When God Winks At You: How God Speaks Directly To You Through the Power of Coincidence by Squire Rushnell
15. Higher is Waiting by Tyler Perry

Soul Purpose Books:

1. GoodGame: The Cheatcode to Betting on Yourself and Living a Purpose-Filled Life on Purpose by Charlie Bingham

2. Start with Why: How Great Leaders Inspire Everyone to Take Action by Simon Sinek

3. Find Your Why by Simon Sinek

4. The 4 Agreements by Don Miguel Ruiz and Janet Mills

5. The 5th Agreement by Don Miguel Ruiz & Don Jose Ruiz

6. Peak Secrets from the New Science of Expertise by Anders Ericsson and Robert Pool

7. The Confident Mind by Dr. Nate Zinsser

8. The Good Life by Robert Waldinger, MD and Marc Schulz PhD

9. How to Win Friends & Influence People in the Digital Age by Dale Carnegie

10. The Happiness Pursuit: Finding the Quest That Will Bring Purpose to Your Life by Chris

11. The Power of Moments by Chip & Dan Heath

12. The 50th Law by Robert Greene & 50 Cent

13. Seeing What Others Don't by Gary Klein

14. Originals: How Non-Conformists Move the World by Adam M. Grant

15. The Art & Science of Respect: A Memoir by James Prince

16. The 10X Rule by Grant Cardone

17. Hit Refresh by Satya Nadella
18. The Alchemist by Paulo Coelho
19. Warrior of the Light by Paulo Coelho
20. The Pilgrimage by Paulo Coelho
21. The Archer by Paulo Coelho
22. Three Magic Words by Uell S. Anderson
23. Learned Optimism by Martin E.P. Seligman PhD
24. The Mountain is You by Brianna West
25. Blueprint: The Evolutionary Origins of a Good Society by Nicholas A. Christakis

Financial Books:

1. The Richest Man in Babylon by George S. Clason
2. Think and Grow Rich by Napoleon Hill
3. Rich Dad Poor Dad by Robert T. Kiyosaki
4. What would the Rockefellers Do?: How the Wealthy Get and Stay That Way, and How You Can Too by Garret B. Gunderson
5. The Power of Zero by David McKnight
6. Money Master the Game by Tony Robbins
7. The Laser Fund by Douglas Andrew
8. Never Split the Difference: Negotiating As If Your Life Depended On It by Chris Voss
9. We Should All Be Millionaires by Rachel Rodgers
10. The Seven Spiritual Laws of Success by Deepak Chopra
11. Hustle Harder by Curtis Jackson

Entrepreneurship Books:

1. Smartcuts: How Hackers, Innovators and Icons Accelerate Success by Simon Sinek
2. The Inevitable: Understanding the 12 Technological Forces That Will Shape Our Future by Kevin Kelly
3. Good to Great by Jim Collins
4. The 7 Habits of Highly Effective People by Stephen R. Covey
5. Contagious: Why Things Catch On by Jonah Berger
6. The 22 Immutable Laws of Marketing: Violate Them At Your Own Risk by Al Ries and Jack Trout
7. The 22 Immutable Laws of Branding: How to Build a Product or Service Into a World Class Brand by Al Ries and Jack Trout
8. The Third Wave: An Entrepreneur's Vision of the Future by Steve Case
9. The Lean Startup by Eric Ries
10. The $100 Startup by Chris Guillebeau
11. Side Hustle: From Idea to Income in 27 Days by Chris Guillebeau
12. Zero to One: Notes on Startups, or How to Build the Future by Peter Thiel
13. The Power of Broke by Draymond John
14. The Art of the Start by Guy Kawasaki
15. Crushing It by Gary Vaynerchuk
16. Getting to Yes: Negotiating Agreement Without Giving In by Roger Fisher
17. The Way of the Wolf by Jordan Belfort

18. AI Superpowers: China, Silicon Valley and the New World Order by Kai-Fu Lee

Relationship Books:

1. Drama Free: A Guide to Managing Unhealthy Family Relationships by Nedra Glover Tawwab
2. Boundaries: When To Say Yes How to Say No by Dr. Henry Cloud & Dr. John Townsend
3. Being the Dad I Never Had: Lifelong Lessons for Fathering After Fatherlessness by Dr. David R. Inniss
4. The Laws of Human Nature by Robert Greene
5. 21 Lessons for the 21st Century by Yuval Noah Harari
6. The Art of Seduction by Robert Grene
7. 48 Laws of Power by Robert Greene
8. Mastery by Robert Greene
9. The Way of the Superior Man: A Spiritual Guide to Mastering the Challenges of Women, Work and Sexual Desire by David Deida
10. The 5 Love Languages: The Secret to Love That Lasts by Gary Chapman
11. Men Are From Mars, Women Are From Venus: The Classic Guide to Understanding the Opposite Sex by John Gray Ph.D.
12. The Love Dare by Alex Kendrick
13. Sacred Marriage: What If God Designed Marriage to Make Us Holy More Than to Make Us Happy? by Gary Thomas
14. Talking to Strangers by Malcolm Gladwell

15. Loving Your Spouse When You Feel Like Walking Away by Gary Chapman
16. Pimpology: The 48 Laws of the Game by Pimpin' Ken
17. The Mind of a MACK: Masculine Articulate & Charismatic King by The Professor of Pimpology
18. The Art of Witty Banter: Be Clever, Quick & Magnetic (How to be More Likable and Charismatic) by Patrick King

Leadership & Career Development Books:

1. Leaders Eat Last by Simon Sinek
2. The First 90 Days: Proven Strategies for Getting Up to Speed Faster and Smarter by Michael D. Watkins
3. Surrounded by Idiots by Thomas Erikson
4. Range by David Epstein
5. What Got You Here Won't Get You There by Marshall Goldsmith
6. FIRE: How Fast, Inexpensive, Restrained, and Elegant Methods Ignite Innovation by Dan Ward
7. Essentialism by Greg McKeown
8. Think Again by Adam Grant
9. Thinking Fast and Slow by Daniel Kahneman
10. 9 Lies About Work by Marcus Buckingham
11. Go Put Your Strengths to Work by Marcus Buckingham
12. The Invisible Gorilla: How Our Intentions

Deceive Us by Christopher Chabris and Daniel Simons

Racial History Books:

1. The Royal Kingdoms of Ghana, Mali and Songhay: Life in Medieval Africa by Patricia McKissack & Frederick McKissack

2. The Isis Papers by Dr. Frances Cress Welsing

3. Destruction of Black Civilization: Great Issues of a Race from 4500 B.C. to 2000 A.D. by Chancellor Williams

4. Stolen Legacy: Greek Philosophy is Stolen Egyptian Philosophy by George G.M. James

5. Caste: The Origins of Our Discontent by Isabela Wilkerson

6. The 1619 Project: A New Origin Story by Nikole Hannah-Jones

7. Colonial Times to the Present by Harriet A. Washington

8. The Color of Law by Richard Rothstein

9. The New Jim Crow by Michelle Alexander

10. Medical Apartheid: The Dark History of Medical Experimentation on Black Americans from

11. The Black Tax: The Cost of Being Black in America by Shawn D. Rochester

12. The Mis-Education of the Negro by Carter G. Woodson Ph.D.

13. The Souls of Black Folk by W.E.B. Du Bois

14. The Fire Next Time by James Baldwin

15. Notes on a Native Son by James Baldwin

16. Black Men, Obsolete, Single, Dangerous?: The Afrikan American Family in Transition by Haki R. Madhubuti

17. Cool Pose: The Dilemmas of Black Manhood in America by Richard Majors & Janet Mancini Billson

18. Raising Black Boys by Dr. Jawanza Kunjufu

19. The New World Order by A. Ralph Emerson

20. Behold a Pale Horse by Milton William Cooper

21. Where Do We Go From Here by Martin Luther King

22. Soul on Ice by Eldridge Cleaver

23. I Am Not Your Negro by James Baldwin

24. Race Matters by Cornel West

25. Post Traumatic Slave Syndrome by Joy Degruy

26. Whistling Vivaldi: How Stereotypes Affect Us and What We Can Do by Claude M. Steele

27. We Were 8 Years in Power: An American Tragedy by Ta-Nehisi Coates

28. Between the World and Me by Ta-Nehisi Coates

29. Lies My Teacher Told Me by James Loewen

30. Dumbing Us Down: The Hidden Curriculum of Compulsory Schooling by John Taylor Gatto

31. White Fragility: Why It's So Hard for White People to Talk About Racism by Dr. Robin DiAngelo
32. White Rage: The Unspoken Truth of Our Racial Divide by Carol Anderson
33. How to be an Antiracist by Ibram X. Kendi

Memoirs:

1. The Death of Mr.GoodGame: My Struggle to Get Sober by Charlie Bingham Jr.
2. Pimp by Iceberg Slim
3. The Naked Soul of Iceberg Slim by Iceberg Slim
4. Becoming by Michelle Obama
5. Jay-Z by Michael Eric Dyson
6. The Marathon Don't Stop: The Life and Times of Nipsey Hussle by Rob Kenner
7. The Rose That Grew From Concrete by Tupac Shakur
8. The Light We Carry by Michelle Obama
9. I Am Debra Lee by Debra Lee
10. Where You Are is Not Who You Are by Ursula Burns
11. Finding Me by Viola Davis
12. A Promised Land by Barack Obama
13. The Autobiography of Gucci Mane by Gucci Mane
14. The Butterfly Effect: How Kedrick Lamar

Ignited the Soul of Black America by Marcus J. Moore

15. Hurricanes: A Memoir by Rick Ross

16. Dapper Dan: Made in Harlem: A Memoir by Daniel R. Day

17. The Billion Dollar BET: Robert Johnson and the Inside Story of Black Entertainment Television by Brett Pulley

18. Let Love Have the Last Word by Common

19. 12 Years A Slave by Solomon Northup

20. The Misadventures of Awkward Black Girl by Issa Rae

21. My Grandfather's Son: A Memoir by Clarence Thomas

22. Walking with the Wind: A Memoir of the Movement by John Lewis

23. I Know Why the Caged Bird Sings by Maya Angelou

24. Angela Davis: An Autobiography

25. The Autobiography of Malcolm X by Alex Haley

26. Assata: An Autobiography by Assata Shakur

27. By Any Means Necessary (Malcolm X Speeches and Writings) by Malcolm X

28. Che Guevara: A Revolutionary Life by Jon Lee Anderson

Printed in the USA
CPSIA information can be obtained
at www.ICGtesting.com
LVHW070205061024
792905LV00020B/312